THE CHANNEL WHISPERER

THE
PAUL SYSMANS
CHANNEL
WHISPERER

HOW TO
RECRUIT,
MANAGE AND
DEVELOP YOUR
DISTRIBUTORS

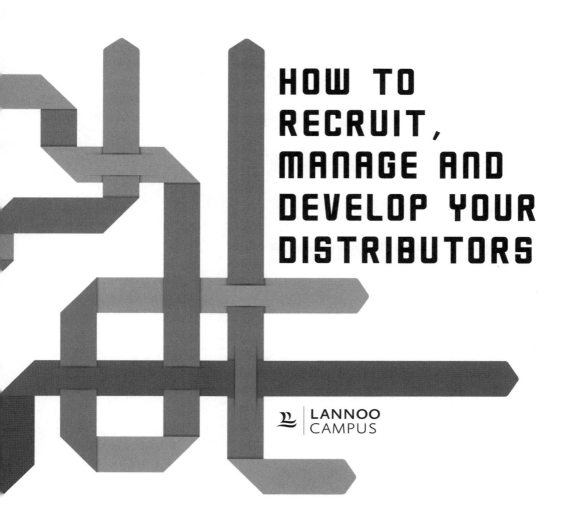

LANNOO
CAMPUS

D/2018/45/64 – ISBN 978 94 014 5047 8 – NUR 800, 801

Cover design: Gert Degrande | De Witlofcompagnie
Interior design: Wendy De Haes

LannooCampus Publishers is a subsidiary of Lannoo Publishers,
the book and multimedia division of Lannoo Publishers nv.

LannooCampus Publishers
Erasme Ruelensvest 179 box 101
3001 Leuven
Belgium
www.lannoocampus.com

TABLE OF CONTENTS

PREFACE

I have always wondered why authors need to thank so many people in
their preface. Now that I've written my very first book, I absolutely get it.
Writing a book makes you realize how many people have an influence on the
knowledge that you want to share with others. From a business perspective
you owe so much to the better managers that you worked for. You learn from
them. Ironically, you should also give credit to the worst ones you worked for
because you learn from them as well. And a lot of credit goes to your relatives.
My wife and children have supported me through my entire career. They have
managed perfectly well by themselves the many days that I was travelling and
the many times that I came home late from meetings and business diners.

But this book also alerted me to the fact that there are other authors – some
of them even true gurus – that have shown me the way, that have provided
structure to my thought process and have inspired me throughout my career.
I hope I can leave you with a similar feeling of joy and excitement after
closing this book.

I want to mention a few authors and celebrities in particular, some of which I
had the pleasure of meeting in person.

Cesar Millan (presenter of *The Dog Whisperer*) was the inspiration to the
title of my book. If you are familiar with his reality show, then you may have
realized by now that when people want to change the behaviour of their
dogs, the key to a positive result does not lay with the dog but with the dog
owners themselves. When companies like yours want to get more out of
your distributors, you should not try to change your distributors but you
should start with changing your own behaviour, your actions and the way you
manage your distributors.

Jan Flamend and Peter Tans (consultants in value based selling). Jan and Peter, both Belgian authors of successful books and consulting activities on the topics of value based selling and many other topics, taught me the basics of value based selling. They made me realize that companies spend, at best, time on developing value propositions for their end-users and how you can best do this. But after speaking to them I know that only few to none of the companies like yours, ever even think about their value proposition to their distributors. Why should distributors work for you? What is in it for them? Or still, how do you deserve your spot, your share of mind and share of their wallet in all the activities that your distributors can choose from?

Jos Burgers (author of *Geef nooit korting! – Never Give a Discount!*). Jos is a Dutch author and speaker. I had the pleasure of joining one of his seminars on how to never "give" discounts. It helped me understand how to maximize prices and margins to distributors. Jos helped me see how I could spend my sales time more wisely when trying to maximize my profit margins. Price negotiations are a game that you can easily win, if you understand the rules.

Simon Sinek (author of *It Starts with Why*). It only took a 15 minutes Tedx talk on YouTube to sensitize me for the mistakes we all make when presenting our products to our distributors and to end-customers. People do not buy from you for what you do. The reason they buy from you is because of the "why" you do it. Still, we like to mainly talk about *what* we do and *how* we do it. But it must start with *why*. Why are you doing what you do? What are you solving for your distributors and their end-users? Only then you should explain to them how you do it and what exactly you do to achieve all of this. Just reverse the order and you will manage to sell your products and services for their true value.

John Cleese (SPIN). Most of you know John Cleese from his acting work in *Monty Python* and *Fawlty Towers* and so many other funny performances. But John Cleese also created some interesting and entertaining sales training videos. One of them, unfortunately hard to find online, has been very inspiring to me. It was on how to stop talking and start listening. In a funny but realistic way the video made me understand how we, sales people, like to spend most of our time talking ourselves and we rarely listen and let our customer or distributor talk. The video made clear how you and I miss many opportunities when trying to understand what adds value to our distributors and end-customers by talking too much and not letting the others speak. The SPIN listening skills will also help you in changing the way you interact with your B2B customers.

Chip and Dan Heath (authors of *Made to Stick: Why Some Ideas Survive and Others Die*). Today's successful communication is based more than ever on storytelling. The best way to sell is by having others sell it for you, since they are more trustworthy than you, the vendor. But good stories must meet a set of criteria to survive and stick. I have been inspired by the book *Made to Stick*. In my chapter on building a value proposition to your distributors, I will briefly explain how the acronym "SUCCESs" in this book is a big help when putting together convincing stories in your marketing communication and when editing your value proposition.

A word of thanks also goes to **Kluwer Opleidingen** and to the **Institute For Business Development (IFBD)**. Both are renowned Belgian training institutes that have given me their confidence since 2012 while performing management training sessions for them on the topic of distributor management a few times per year. The trainees have inspired me to take the time to write this book. They made me realize that hardly any literature on distributor management was available until now.

And last but not least, a special thanks to publishing company **LannooCampus**. As a rookie author I had the pleasure of being surrounded by people that have guided me through the publishing process in a professional and enjoyable way. Thank you for your confidence and your trust.

After my consulting or training sessions with companies, many people came up to me and told me they knew the basics of what I had shared with them, but they all admitted that until then they were missing the structured approach and execution plan, the template to really make it all happen in their own company. This is the little dream that I have with my book. I hope that you do not only get the necessary building blocks to build or optimize your own channel house, but more importantly, that you go out tomorrow and finally start doing it.

March 2018

INTRODUCTION

Those of you who are in training or consultancy know that today's training approach is no longer based on one-directional teaching, but on sharing, learning from others, exchanging thoughts and experiences between trainees. With more than thirty years of experience in international B2B sales and marketing management in different industries, both with multinational as well as smaller size companies, I believe to have developed a vision on distributor management that was worth sharing. How can you get more out of your distributors, rather than being frustrated about their lack of performance, continuous request for better prices and more support?

Through my management training sessions and by listening to my trainees I have learned that most companies are facing the same challenges with their distributors. So whichever industry you are in, the basics of how to optimize your distribution channel strategy will apply. My own experience is mainly built on the international sales and marketing of capital equipment and services in a B2B environment. If you are more into retail and B2C business, I still appreciate that you purchased this book and I hope it will inspire you.

FORGET ABOUT CHANNEL DEFINITIONS

You would expect me to start this book by extensively explaining the differences between distributors, dealers, wholesalers, agents, retailers and more. But no, I will not steel your valuable time for something that is widely available on the Internet. In this book I will refer to the general word **"distributors"** for any channel partner that is buying product or services from you with the purpose of selling and supporting it to end-users. They all share the interest and purpose of generating profit with your products and services. I am sure that you will forgive me this shortcut.

Although I am aware of the sometimes significant differences between all of the channel types, my focus in this book will be on the business relationship with your existing and potential channel partners. The only rail changer at which we will make a short stop, is the question whether you should sell directly to your end-users or choose a deviation to the indirect channels track. Other than that I will continue to refer to all of the B2B channel partners as your "distributors" from here on.

THE BUILDING BLOCKS TO DISTRIBUTOR SUCCESS

Getting the most out of your distributors is based on three major building blocks, all of which I will cover in chronological order in this book.

RECRUIT
MANAGE
DEVELOP

You may already be working with distributors today, but no doubt you believe that too many are not performing to your full satisfaction. You bought my book for a reason. Whichever of the three building blocks your focus may be on today, it is always worth checking how you can optimize the other ones as well. All three building blocks are crucial parts of the foundation to successful distributor management. If you have a weakness in one of them, your channel house may collapse.

THE COMPLAINTS WE ALL SHARE

With some level of arrogance, I dare to state that you have the same complaints as many of your peers. My training courses always start with the question "What are your most important complaints about your distributors?". Before reading the next paragraph, maybe write them down for yourself and then check below.

Here's what usually makes it to the flip chart:

- » They do not execute our strategy.
- » They are not performing well enough.
- » They are not spending enough time on our products.
- » They always try to negotiate prices.
- » They need too much support from us.
- » They always want exclusivity.
- » They create channel conflicts.
- » And more...

WHAT THIS BOOK IS ABOUT

Cesar Millan, the dog whisperer, helps people in making their naughty dogs obey and have them execute what the pack leaders, the owners, want. Or to be more exact: he trains the pack leaders on how to act differently to make the change happen.

Well, my approach in getting the most out of your distributors is no different. This book will take you in chronological order through all the important steps that it takes to develop a relationship with your channels that makes them work a lot harder for you. It deals in the first place with what YOU can do differently, by understanding better what THEY want and expect from you. It also deals with how you can turn your distributors from a customer that you try to serve today into an extension of your company that supports you and enjoys working with you as their preferred vendor.

WHO CAN BENEFIT FROM THIS BOOK?

When writing this book, I have always had multiple target readers in mind. My focus has mainly been on anybody working in an international but also national B2B environment. I wanted it to be valuable not only to experienced, but also to novice channel managers. I wanted it to be useful for companies already working with distributors as well as companies starting their development process outside of their home market. General managers, sales managers, marketing managers, account managers, all of you will hopefully benefit from this book.

The more the book advanced and the more I started sharing parts of it with some of my business contacts, the more I started to realize that many distributors themselves would definitely be interested in offering the book to their suppliers as a gift. Well, I certainly won't try to talk them out of that, and I suspect neither will my publisher.

BOARD AT YOUR NEAREST STATION

I have tried to rank all relevant topics in a way that wherever you and your company are in the process of recruiting new or managing existing distributors, you can step in wherever you want. Depending on the progress you have already made, you can focus on any individual chapter in the book. However, I suggest that you board at the starting station all the same. I am convinced that you will still discover weak spots in your channel strategy that deserve and need further optimization.

WHAT YOU CAN EXPECT

Let me set the expectations right. I cannot bring you paradise, but I hope that after reading this book you will at least see it from here. The reason that there is no guarantee for success is because you still need the right staff to implement it all and you need distributors that show the willingness to grow with you as well. Unfortunately, that is not always the case, with some of your distributors being perfectly happy with where they are today. But also for the hardheads among your distributors, I hope this book holds a recipe for change.

Let me shed some light on the chronological approach of this book, on the train stations that we will make a stop at and why we do plan to make stops there.

Too many companies decide to conquer national or international markets without their corporate strategy well in place. Let us be clear, distributors are not an easy solution to a lack of strategic vision or lack of understanding of your target markets. Without the necessary investment in collecting market intelligence, performing market segmentation and understanding what brings value to these target segments, your plan is doomed to fail. Strategic planning is not only the mentioning of numbers that you dream about, it is all about the execution of your plan. Strategy is a journey and it can sometimes be one with a lot of unexpected obstacles that require revisions of the plan.

A good business plan will make it a lot easier for you to develop your supporting marketing strategy afterwards. One important topic within your marketing plan is your channel strategy. It is one of the famous 4 Ps (Place) in Jerome McCarthy's initial and simple to use 4 Ps marketing mix (Product – Price – Place – Promotion).

RECRUIT

Too many companies walk into the opportunism trap when bringing new distributors on board. In general, not enough time is spent on a clear definition of the desired distributor profile and therefore too many of the new distributorships are showing disappointing sales results. But this can be avoided.

After you have found your new partner, should you sign a distributor agreement or not? If you decide to do so, at least make it the right one from the very start. Too many companies would like to see their contracts changed because too much was given away too fast in their distributor agreements.

Equally important as recruiting the right distributors is the recruitment of the right sales staff. Sales managers dealing with a large network of distributors, national or international, are Premier League players in my opinion. They are managing a very large team of sales people in a usually large geographical region. The distributor's sales people are not reporting directly to you or your sales manager and they are also not on your payroll. Making them work for you to your expectation therefore requires advanced sales skills, which unfortunately many do not have. I have been there myself and will share with you what I believe that it takes for the job.

MANAGE

We are often too focused on our end-customers and forget about the maybe even most important asset, our distributors. Many, if not most customers buy in the first place because of their trust in your distributor, not because of your products or services. Be aware of this.

The basics of value selling will help you understand why customers, but also your distributors, buy or don't buy from you. Understanding value based selling will help you understand the importance of developing your team's listening skills. They can and should be educated on how to sell differently to your end-users and to your distributors. And maybe even more important, I will reveal some tips and tricks on how to make your distributors and yourself make more profit margin this way. And increased margin is what drives your distributors. This is what will make them work harder for you.

Price negotiations are one of my favourite topics. Accountants often spend hours calculating cost prices down to the eurocent. And then us, the so-called best sales people on the planet, give that one percent extra discount way too easily and without realizing how much it affects our bottom line. What a pity. I will share with you how you can change the mind of your sales team and no longer give away unnecessary discounts to your distributors and your end-users. Like many of your peers, you may be wondering what a fair margin to your distributor should look like and why.

You will also learn that your true competitors are not the standard brand names that come to your mind when I ask you. You have other hidden competitors that determine your success rate when selling through distributors. Not market share but in the first place share of wallet and share of mind should become your focus from here on.

DEVELOP

Finding and having strong distributors in place is one thing, developing them to the next level is an even bigger challenge. Most important when working with distributors, is the creation of a different mindset. Distributors are not just your customers. They should also be an extension of your organization. They work for you and you pay them for that work with a reasonable distributor margin. Like you do with your own staff, you should give them targets. You must coach, train and reward them. If they do not perform well, be more assertive and do not lose valuable time while just hoping that maybe next year they will do better. Of course you will hear that the market is so tough this year, competition is more aggressive than ever. Fighting this, again requires high level sales skills.

Next to an extension of your organization they are indeed also valuable customers that deserve your highest level of respect. Measure their satisfaction more often and improve your business processes with them where possible. With the value selling skills that this book will help you develop, you will be able to discover yourself what truly adds value to your distributors. You will hopefully get inspired to try and find out how you can make their tasks easier and more successful. You will learn to better understand their gains and pains as a distributor and respond to it with a better distributor value proposition.

And last but not least, I will take you through the necessary separation process from distributors. Terminating distributor relationships is sometimes inevitable, but the process is often postponed way too long. The decision to do so should be taken more often and more quickly but requires careful thinking and full upper management support. I will elaborate in this book on how to minimize the potential negative impact on your sales results when taking the courageous decision to divorce from any distributor.

Our journey starts here.

1

DEVELOPING
A CHANNEL STRATEGY

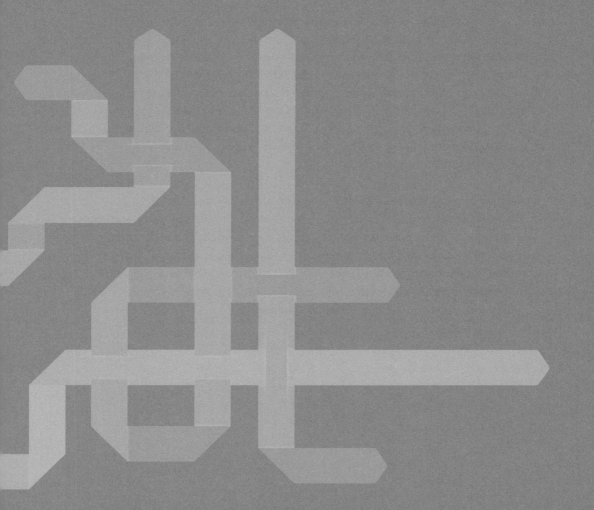

During my entire career I have experienced how difficult it is for managers to get a good quality strategic plan in place. Some claim they don't have time for it or even worse, that they don't see the added value. "The business is happening today", is their most common excuse. The development and execution of a strategic plan is a journey. You know that hurdles will pop up on the road to success. You will need to take deviations here and there. All of that is true, but not defining where you want to go and not communicating clearly to your team what your vision is and how you plan to get where you want to be, is asking for trouble and may paralyze your entire organization.

I won't spend much time on how to make the best strategic business plans. There are hundreds of books and "how to" articles available on the Web on this topic. What I do want to cover, are those sections of the strategic business plan that I think really matter to your planned distributor management improvement program.

Failing to plan is planning to fail.
– Alan Lakein

For convenience, let us choose the following simplified template as a chronological guideline and work together from there. The general objective of the strategic business plan is to define where you want to be in a number of years from now and how you believe you will be able to achieve that ambition.

- » Vision
- » Mission
- » Company and business
- » Market
- » Marketing plan
- » Competition
- » SWOT analysis
- » Organization
- » Operational plan
- » Financial plan

Most templates include more topics, but I deliberately keep it basic and limited to the most relevant chapters. It is better to focus at least on these few than not doing any strategic planning at all.

Vision

If you want to inspire distributors to work harder for you, do not limit yourself to just mentioning how much revenue the CEO wants to achieve in three to five years from now. To them that number is just somebody else's dream and it will not excite them. Why would they care? However, if you share with your distributors a promising and credible vision on what you think is going on out there in the market, if you share which opportunities you see on the horizon and which potential profit it may generate for all of you, then you will get their attention.

That inspiration and excitement should not only be shared with your distributors but also with your own staff. You can't expect magic if you don't inspire the company staff which deals with your distributors every day. Or as author, motivational speaker and marketing consultant Simon Sinek put it in a tweet:

> Customers will never love a company
> until the employees love it first.
>
> — Simon Sinek

Your staff and distributors will never love your company and work hard for it because of the ambitious revenue target of the CEO. They will love it for the vision that your company shares, for the trust that you show in seeing something that hopefully other vendors don't see. They will love you and embrace you for having ideas that can potentially generate a bright future for all of you. That is why vision matters.

It takes only four minutes of your time to understand what I mean. Go to http://bit.ly/1F1SQgO and watch John F. Kennedy's speech to Congress on May 25, 1961 in which he asks for the funding of NASA's space program. According to Kennedy, America had to play a leading role in securing peace around the world. It could do so by requiring a dominant position in space. Therefor the nation's mission was to put a man on the moon and bring him back safely to earth before the end of the decade.

If you were a NASA staff member in 1961, how could you not get excited over working for the space program in those next years until the end of the decade? That's how you develop motivation. That's how you find partnering distributors and a driven team that are willing to work hard for you.

Mission

A lot of discussion exists on what a good mission statement should look like. I like to refer to it as "the marching orders for the troops". And as I will explain further, your distributors are not only your customers. They are part of your troops and should be handled and instructed as such. They should not act like volunteers that can decide to join some of your operations one time and step out from or be less active at their convenience and discretion in the ones they like less. But this means that you as a company have to be very clear on where you want them to go next and what role you expect everyone to play in achieving your objectives. Just saying that you will meet them at the top of the mountain, is generally not going to lead to the success that you are hoping for.

In your vision statement you predict what will happen, what you hope to find at a certain place and time in the market in the future. The mission statement on the other hand should help all stakeholders to understand how you want to get to that promising market spot. It is the road that you jointly chose to take, the track you want everyone to agree upon and to follow in the climb. If your distributors are not on that same mission, you should not be surprised that some do not show up at the agreed meeting point at the agreed time. They may have encountered obstacles and chosen other more interesting routes or may have dropped out without telling you. I generally refer to it as still taking orders from their customers, but not selling anymore.

Once again, do not lose valuable time in exploring the exact difference between vision and mission. Focus on developing a message, an inspiration to your team and to your distributors, that makes it clear what you believe in, what you expect to happen to your market, why that is and how we can all benefit from this. Just inspire.

Company and business

This section of your business plan should cover the nature of your business. Seek confirmation with your distributors on what drives your and their business. Which are the external factors that may influence the mission that you have defined? A current example is the impact of low oil prices on the Middle East business potential for many companies. Who are the customers that you are selling to, the end-users? Who are the decision makers in the buying process? How do your customers generally acquire your products or services? Which kind of training and support do your customers expect? Which trends do you see in the customer expectations and e.g. in the logistic processes? For me this is another important box that needs to be ticked early in your strategic planning process. Failing to do so may cost valuable time in developing and executing the rest of the plan with your internal and external stakeholders not coming to an agreement on the marketing planning and other key topics due to disagreement on the basics of your industry and your business.

Market

Why are you in this business? Why does this market need your products or services? Which market segments are you or should you be addressing? Where do you see most of the opportunities? The Boston Consulting Group Matrix, Product Market Mixes, MaBa Matrices (Market Attractiveness/ Business Attractiveness) and other tools can help you define the most interesting segments for you to focus on. Decide whether you want to play in the high end of the market or rather the value segment with lower prices and with more focus on volume. Look into geographies, demographic segments, application segments. Use any tool that works best for you and your team, but at least go out and do it. Your company's financial means are probably not unlimited. If you are a midsize company, a decision on what you will *not* do, is equally important as deciding which markets you *do* want to penetrate.

Your distributors will prove to be a very important asset in your growth strategy. You have choices to make on where your time and money will probably generate the highest return on investment. Your decisions on the market segments will and should also drive your choice of distributor types. Fail to pick the right segments and partners, and results will be below expectation. Do not blame the distributors in the first place if you did not take the right or even no decision at all on which segments you actually wanted to focus on. The idea that you best randomly shoot all over the place in order to hit something, usually is not the smartest strategy.

The essence of strategy is choosing what not to do.
– Michael Porter

We will also discuss the importance of evaluating your current distributors and bring them to the next level or worst case separate from them if there is no alignment with your segmentation and required distributor profiles. We will extensively talk about distributor profiles but segmentation is one of your key decision parameters on the best profiles, on their physical location, on the number of feet on the street that you will need, and more.

Setting financial targets with your existing or new distributors requires understanding of market size and of competition. Equally important is the knowledge on end-user and distributor market prices in the segments that you are exploring. No price negotiation with distributors will ever work to your benefit if you enter the ring with little to no reliable information on and no understanding of the net market prices. Who are your competitors, what is their value proposition? What is your value added? All of this needs to be carefully evaluated if you want to have a fair chance of maximizing your prices and profit margin. We will cover this extensively later.

Marketing strategy

Developing your market intelligence generally happens in close collaboration with your marketing department and should lead in the end to the popular 4 Ps of the marketing mix, or other model that you prefer. It may be outdated and more Ps have been added in the meantime to the model, but it works fine if you are less experienced with marketing strategy and if you want to keep it simple in your first and basic distributor management improvement initiative.

Allow me to also share with you a very pragmatic selection of topics in a standard marketing plan template that I believe to be the most relevant ones in the process of distributor recruitment, management and development.

>> Target customers (market segmentation)
>> Unique Buying Reasons (previously called USPs)
>> Pricing and positioning (distributor and end-user pricing)
>> Distribution strategy (channel selection)
>> Product portfolio (products and services offering)
>> Marketing materials (marketing tools)
>> Promotions strategy (sales actions)
>> Online marketing strategy (digital marketing)
>> Conversion strategy (lead-to-order)
>> Referral strategy (leverage existing customer base)
>> Retention strategy (keeping existing customers)

TARGET CUSTOMERS (MARKET SEGMENTATION)

Next to influencing your choice of distributors, your market segmentation will also determine how you will communicate to your target audience. Your stories should matter to them. Marketing and sales staff should understand what adds value to each of the stakeholders in each of the segments. They must learn and understand what influences the customer perception. The role of marketing and sales is to help a customer in taking a buying decision. This is exactly what great sales people do. They understand what has value to that one specific customer in front of them and help them in the buying decision process by working on their perception. We will spend several chapters on that process. It applies not only to your end-customers but just as much to your distributors.

UNIQUE BUYING REASONS (PREVIOUSLY CALLED USPS)

More important than discussing whether or not UBRs (Unique Buying Reasons) works better as a name than USPs (Unique Selling Proposition), is the question what really sets you apart from your competition. Why should customers, including your distributors, buy from you and represent you? What justifies your maybe (and hopefully) higher price than the price the competition offers? You want your distributors to be able and deliver that. Not only should your distributors be strongly active in the segments of your choice, they should also be able to deliver the required market expertise, professional end-user training, the after sales support and everything else that you and your company stand for. The UBRs are many times not what you believe them to be. They are way more often to be found with the performance of your distributors than with your own product and services quality. Understand this, see how you can help your distributors in delivering better what the end-users expect, and your business will develop to expectation.

PRICING AND POSITIONING
(DISTRIBUTOR AND END-USER PRICING)

As I will explain in the chapter on distributor margin and pricing, all of the different steps in your pricing strategy play an important role. The list price of your dealer to the end-users supports the positioning of your product against competition. The net end-user price indicates how much "perceived" value you bring to your customers and will, in the end, determine the net margin that a distributor can make.

The net margin will influence largely their interest in actively selling your product, rather than just taking orders. But it will also negatively influence your own profit margins if you just leave the pricing decision to the distributor by lack of market intelligence on your side. You should be in control of the pricing process and developing the necessary market knowledge should help you in getting into the driver seat. Many companies are not maximizing their profit because they put way too much trust in the information that is provided by distributors and because they don't do their homework properly. Just like banks are not there to "help" you when you need money for your new house, distributors also have their own business agenda. You cannot blame them for that. Like you, they are professional and smart business people.

DISTRIBUTION STRATEGY (CHANNEL SELECTION)

Picking the right channels for your product and services is again one of the Ps in the simplified version of the 4 Ps marketing mix, in which this P now stands for "Place".

Many companies decide to work with channel partners as a quick fix for not being able to enter a market with their own direct sales organization. At the same time, you do see organizations at a later stage modify their distribution model back to direct sales through a subsidiary, after business has started to really pick up. In the next chapter I will cover the many reasons why working with distributors can work to your benefit.

PRODUCT PORTFOLIO
(PRODUCTS AND SERVICES OFFERING)

Working with distributors adds an extra dimension to the definition of your products and services portfolio. Not only should you think about the value proposition to your end-users, you should also evaluate your current offering and new developments from the perspective of your distributors. Are your products and services easy for the distributor to acquire, sell and support?

A lot of margin is often lost in the value chain because of not having considered this well enough. What can you maybe do to further lower the cost of getting your products and services to the end-customer? How can you further simplify the use of your machine and reduce this way the time that your distributor needs to schedule for end-user training? How can you change the engineering of your product in a way that it becomes much more cost-efficient for the distributor to replace components in case of a product failure? How can the Internet of Things be used to analyse technical problems faster and avoid that your distributor has to waste valuable time driving many miles to a remote customer a few times before a technical problem gets fixed?

MARKETING MATERIALS (MARKETING TOOLS)

When working with distributors, more than ever you should move away from developing brochures, web pages or anything that focuses on telling what your products or services are about. Your approach should truly become one where you start by asking the question how you can make the distributor more successful. What is the task they are performing as a dealer? What do end-customers expect from the distributor and how can you help as their vendor in creating the correct perception about this? What does the sales process look like and how can your marketing communication generate sparks in the head of the distributor? How can you train and help your distributor in getting more leads from their own website? The list is endless but it starts with a change of your mindset. Move from telling what you normally like to tell about yourself to exploring what your distributors may need to increase their hit rate. After reading the value selling chapter in this book, you will understand.

PROMOTION STRATEGY (SALES ACTIONS)

Sales campaigns serve multiple purposes. If not managed properly, distributors will perceive it in the first place as an opportunity for them to source product cheaper from you, just to store extra product in their warehouse and making a better margin when the next customer stops by at their shop to buy one. That is not what you are after.

Sales campaigns have a much more important value in your channel strategy than this. They should create again another event, another opportunity for your distributors to go out in the field and have a conversation, in the broad sense of the word, with their end-users. It adds to influencing perception and to the creation of "share of mind". It is another spark in the brain of the distributor and it shows your commitment to their market.

When it comes to pricing strategy later in the book, I will try to convince you that discounting in sales campaigns is generally not the best approach. It sends the wrong message, attracts the wrong customers and just costs you profit margin. There are much smarter approaches, as you will learn.

ONLINE MARKETING STRATEGY (DIGITAL MARKETING)

It is vital that you make your distributors understand the changes that are going on in the marketing world. Digitalization, Internet, the move from pushing to pulling information, the increased importance of peers of the customers as their information source, the role of social media in influencing perception. Many of your distributors may not understand much of these developments yet and prefer to run their conversations with end-customers in sometimes outdated style. I have learned that next to getting good product and good product training, offering sales training and marketing training to your distributors, educating them on how to get more out of their own online interaction with their customers, may add tremendous value and drive them to working harder for you and with you.

Ignoring online marketing is like opening a business but not telling anyone.
– www.myfrugalbusiness.com

Next to developing modern tools for interacting with your end-users and your distributors, you also need to define a strategy on how you will get your distributors fully on board in your digital marketing strategy. Building a powerful communication machine requires the inclusion of your distributors in your online strategy. Do not only train them but try to get their full buy-in. In the end, this should lead to them opening up their customer database to you in order to develop conversations directly to end-customers, an improved lead generation process but also a higher exit barrier for those distributors that may consider working less hard for you or even leave you. It leads again to the higher share of mind that we are targeting.

CONVERSION STRATEGY (LEAD-TO-ORDER)

The best way to win your distributors' confidence is by bringing a significant amount of quality sales leads to them. The result of your online marketing strategy should be getting existing and potential customers to "visit" you as a company. Your task is to develop a platform for good lead capturing, lead qualification and lead communication to the distributors. It also becomes a strong management tool that can be used when measuring distributor performance and when benchmarking them against other distributors. We will discuss this further later.

REFERRAL STRATEGY
(LEVERAGE EXISTING CUSTOMER BASE)

Many times distributors are not very willing to share details with you on their customer base and their sales funnel. In general, it is based on a lack of trust in you. With that detailed customer information, you could potentially take over when you decide to change your channel strategy to direct sales. With this attitude and lack of trust, a lot of potential is lost, not only in the digital marketing strategy but also when it comes to using your existing customer base as a reference for the many potential customers that you still have out there.

Reality is that many of your potential customers today check with their peers on their experience and satisfaction with your brand. This also applies to their evaluation of the performance of your distributor. You should develop plans to open that important gate and direct link to the end-users. Developing direct communication with the end-users, having valuable conversations and interactions with them and creating a pull strategy from the end-users towards your distributor, is today what many companies try to achieve. It should help you in getting more control over which messages get delivered to the end-users and how. It generates more alignment between all communication channels that you work on.

Storytelling plays a key role in modern marketing in that respect. The best way to sell your products and services, is by not having to sell it yourself. Potential customers tend to believe other customers more than you, for obvious reasons. Stories from peers – testimonials – are more trustworthy than your sales talks or those from your distributors. Create a platform to make this happen and develop an approach that convinces your distributors to join the process. You will need to educate them on how they will also benefit from this referral strategy in the end.

RETENTION STRATEGY (HOW TO KEEP CUSTOMERS)

All of us know that keeping a customer and trying to sell even more to the same customer, is far more cost-efficient than acquiring new customers. Your role as a vendor is to develop a strategy on how to maximize customer loyalty. This is next to maybe monitoring the performance of your distributors even better and next to setting up an efficient Customer Relationship Management (CRM) system. Embrace your end-customers. Develop the right communication strategy, loyalty programs and smart campaigns that will keep them from even looking at the competition next time they need to buy. This may all sound logical, but only few companies have a formal retention strategy in place. Try to become the one that does have one. It will secure a long term and profitable relationship with your distributors as well.

Competition

Just like the SWOT analysis below, some will claim that competition analysis should be listed under marketing strategy, which is probably correct. The reason I mention it separately is because I want to change your vision in this book on who your true competitors are. When working with distributors the game changes. You should no longer just worry about your direct competitors only, but also about the other products and services that your distributors are offering. You may not understand why your distributor is not more successful against a given competitor, while you have spent so much effort in making the best product in the world and offering the best service to them. You will learn to understand that you are in a fight for "share of wallet" and "share of mind", all within that one and the same distributor. But we will get to this later.

SWOT analysis

If you have managed to get your act together on the previous topics, it is important to still do your SWOT analysis. Some will claim that you need to run this earlier in the process, which you can. But also at this point in the process it is important to repeat the analysis. You want to execute a cross-check on your extensive plan. You want to understand where the risks are for failure, both internal and external. What may require a backup plan? Where may your resources not be sufficient to achieve what you want? Maybe important infrastructure is lacking?

Organization

I have put organization or human resources in this late phase of the strategic planning process because it should support the plan and not the other way around. Many organizations build their plan around the resources they currently have. When you have clearly defined your channel strategy, your portfolio, the services you want to offer to your end-customers but also to your distributors, then you should go back to the drawing board and paint the ideal organization to support all of this. It should start with processes, roles and responsibilities, in blank boxes. Only then you start filling out the names of the people you have today. Some boxes may remain blank and some of the existing names may not end up in any of the boxes. However social your company may be, have the courage to take tough decisions where needed. Some of your staff may fit better in other responsibilities, and you should only go for the best. You deserve it, but so do your distributors. You want to inspire them. You want them to work harder for you. Then show them leadership and give them what they need and even deserve. Play Major League.

Operational plan

It is all about execution. Discussing your strategy is tough, but execution is what really matters of course. Execution is the uphill battle.

I will invite you in this book to start looking at your distributors in two different ways. They are customers of yours – even important ones – but they are also an extension of your organization. Like you do with your own staff, they should present to you their "sales activity plans", as I will call them later. Their scheduled initiatives in the next period should be shared with you. Not only does it bring your sales meetings with them to a higher level, it also helps you in understanding how you can support them better. It helps in creating strategy and execution alignment, but also creates mutual respect. Your business just cannot depend on the discretion of the distributor, on what their personal plans and ambitions are. If you want them to work hard for you, then you need to ask for their detailed planning related to your products and consolidate it with your plans for that region. Lead, manage and develop the relationship.

Strategy without tactics is the slowest route to victory.
– Sun Tzu, The Art of War

Financial plan

This one speaks for itself, I believe. You want to translate your plans into numbers. To measure is to know. But related to distributors I will encourage you to organize a more formal communication to them on your business objectives for the full year and even by quarter. I will also recommend you, if you haven't done this already, to organize regular and also formal communication on their results and overall performance. If done properly, it will help your account managers in having the right discussions with your distributors, with a better balance of power and not only limited to having to hear where you failed again in the past months. But numbers alone will not do the job. As you will notice in one of the next chapters, I attach great importance to recruiting best in class account managers. Only few are able to handle this sometimes hard power game.

Although I realize that this is a very condensed version of strategic business planning, I hope it has still made you aware of the importance of strategic planning when you are serious about recruitment, management and development of your distributors.

With an optimized corporate and channel strategy in place, let us now discuss which type of sales people I believe you need to make it all happen.

2

HIRING AND IMPROVING YOUR SALES STAFF

The quest for Clark Kent

As you will experience throughout this book, I put a high value on the position of the B2D (Business to Distributor) Managers. Companies like yours, working with national or international distributors, should invest heavily in hiring the right profiles for this job. Doing business with distributors is playing Premier League soccer. It requires a set of skills from your sales people that only few out there really master.

Great B2D Managers are not a cost to your company. They are an investment that can generate a significantly higher profit margin, as I will try to show you in the next chapters. Let us just mention value based selling and price negotiations as two of maybe the most important ones. I will share what I believe to be the profiles you should look for and how to evaluate, coach and grow the B2D managers that you may have working for you today.

B2D managers in my definition are sales managers that are responsible for the management and development of a usually large team of sales people, many times international, that have different cultural backgrounds, have their own business agenda, are not on your payroll and are not even reporting to you. What a challenge. Those of you who have a management responsibility today, know how tough it is already to be a good and inspiring manager to the people that are part of your own company. So how much tougher is it not to drive and manage the ones that are not part of your organization? It is like raising the kids of another family while their parents are standing next to them, invisible to you, and still telling them what they should do next, still feeding them and still giving them a warm place to stay. B2D managers are like adoption parents that have little to nothing to offer to their foster children but still want them to execute everything they ask for. Well, it takes award winning parents to achieve this and they are a rare breed.

The role of your B2D manager is to "embrace" your distributors as if they were his or her own children. Make them feel welcome, give them warmth, create happiness and offer them a home that they enjoy staying at. They want to feel progress. They need to be able to trust you.

But at the same time you need to enforce your house rules, to convey what should be done, just making them do what you want without trying to just enforce it on them. I will refer to this further on as looking at the distributors through two different lenses. On the one hand the distributors are your *customers*, which you need to embrace and keep happy. But on the other hand, they are also an *extension of your company*. They need to do their homework, achieve results and do what you want them to do. It takes a Clark Kent, yes indeed, a Superman profile and exceptional skills from a B2D manager to comply with this unique combination. There are super heroes out there that manage to do it, but only a few. It is your job to find the best ones. Not just you but also your distributors deserve it and you will both benefit from it.

What makes it extra hard to find the right people is that you are dealing with sales people. Ask any recruiter and they will confirm that sales people are good at selling themselves. So it requires professionals to separate the wheat from the chaff. Since you may be the one that will be briefing the recruiters, I will try to give you a set of important skills that a B2D manager should master in my opinion.

You don't need crocodiles

Crocodiles have very big mouths and very small ears. This is exactly what you *don't* need in your B2D management. You do not need the hard selling type of sales people but rather ones that have developed strong listening skills, who bring market and industry experience with them and so much more. But at the same time they need to be able to close deals, to make distributors come to decisions rather than them listening forever to what your company is still missing in your portfolio, that the market is so tough and that you are just too expensive. You need a good balance between the B2C very convincing sales person and the consultative selling OEM/project type of sales person. So, which profile do you need then?

Looking for Mr & Mrs FINE

The *finest* sales people to distributors are a combination of four main characteristics, which are covered by the following "FINE" acronym that I always like to use:

Facilitator
  » is able to convey your company's strategy to the distributors
  » continuously inspires the distributors to work hard for your company
  » creates what we will later call "share of mind" within a distributor team
  » takes ownership over the business relationship and follows up what matters
  » gets things done from your own team members in the organization

Integrator
  » aligns the strategy of your company with the one of the distributor
  » imposes successfully your business processes onto the distributor
  » seeks smart solutions for deviations from the standard business processes

---

Negotiator

- » masters negotiation skills in general (not limited to price negotiations)
- » defends the interest of both your company and that of the distributor
- » has negotiation power (within given boundaries)
- » maximizes profit by not choosing the road of the least resistance (discounting)
- » sets targets, manages and coaches the distributor as if they were direct reports
- » creates interest inside your company for business opportunities with distributors
- » defends the interest of the distributor inside your company with valid arguments
- » convinces management to respond to relevant distributor requests

Expert

- » shows industry, market segments, technical and competition intimacy
- » understands the value added of your company's offering
- » turns each distributor contact into another event
- » identifies business opportunities for the distributor
- » understands what distributors need to be more successful in their tasks

Allow me to summarize the above still differently in my favourite list of ten key words, let's say characteristics that you should try to check yourself when interviewing your next candidate for a potential B2D management position. Or, at least use them in your briefing to the recruitment agency.

» **Strategic** (able to articulate the company's strategy and values, able to understand and translate distributor needs into opportunities)

» **Value seller** (listening skills and able to convey your end-customer and distributor value proposition)

» **Industry expert** (familiar with the business environment, eager to learn)

» **Self-starter** (results driven with good time management and priority setting)

» **Negotiator**

» **Communicator**

» **Team player** (able to motivate people in your company to work for them)

» **Flexible** (able to work with different distributor profiles and unexpected situations)

» **Solutions-oriented** (getting things done)

» **Social and networking skills** (business development, identifying additional distributors)

Money talks

If you are wondering still how to best incentivize your B2D sales staff, then my recommendation is a compensation program based on profit margin.

In general sales people are strongly driven by a good bonus program. However, too many companies put one in place that is not aligned to their company strategy. If your company is driven by increase of the profit margin, then incentivize your team based on the same targets. Many companies prefer not to share cost information with their team, but you do not automatically have to. It is perfectly possible to create a bonus program that shows the net result for the sales people without having to reveal all of that confidential information.

On the other hand, I believe – but this is my personal opinion – that B2D managers should be given some inside in cost prices and product margins, so they can work out proposals to distributors themselves that will maximize profit. I like to refer to the chapter in this book on distributor margin and on price negotiations with distributors. Empower your B2D managers. If you can't trust them with cost information, they may not be the right people for the job.

Your margin based bonus scheme will reward sales people that do not take the road of the least resistance. It incentivizes the ones that have the courage to say "no" to the distributors in the next unjustified price discussion, or "can't do" to that next standard marketing budget support that is being requested. Create a win-win situation in which you share your profit with your sales staff. It will make them work harder for you and keep them happy.

Your company's success however is generally a team effort, so don't neglect the people that contributed to the distributors' business success. A small one-time bonus can do miracles and recognition is the key word here. But those who have accepted the risk of a high variable income also deserve the biggest upside when targets are exceeded. A bonus cap that avoids exorbitantly high variable income remains recommended. You want your sales person to still be happy next year, don't you?

But remember most of all that the position and profile of the B2D manager is highly underestimated. Companies too often go with the second best while you need Premier League players in your distributor business. It is a strategic game in which your counterparts, the distributors, have developed strong negotiation skills and are better informed than ever before through the online communication world that we live in. Your company needs top class B2D managers and the distributors deserve them.

3
RECRUITING YOUR DISTRIBUTORS

You have clearly defined your strategic priorities. The distribution strategy is set and understood. All stakeholders have received clear communication on where the ship is heading and why. You have also put a great sales team together or you have at least built a plan on how to bring your current team to the next level. (And giving them a copy of this book was actually one of your better ideas.) Congratulations on that. It is time now to initiate your quest for great distributors that can make it all happen "for" you and "with" you, either on a national or an international level. Let us, next to recruiting new distributors, also try to find an answer to the question on how you can make your current distributors work harder for you.

The following must sound familiar to you. You are at your impressive booth at this one very important international tradeshow. You are chatting with one of your colleagues. Since many years you have dreamt of one day getting a market position in Turkey. And suddenly... out of nowhere your Prince Charming appears (feel free to imagine it's a princess). He or she sits on a white horse, is potentially surrounded by servants that are there to impress but keep silent. He walks straight to you and speaks the mesmerizing words: "I am by far the largest distributor of the whole of Turkey, from north to south and from east to west. I can turn your brand into the leading brand in Turkey in no time, based on my strong reputation. All I need from you is a bit of exclusivity and prices that are way below what you probably planned on giving me in the first place."

You run to your General Manager and make the famous Obama statement: "We've got him." And before you know it, you have signed an exclusive agreement to find out, just a few weeks later already, that it is not exactly your dream come true. The starting order is highly disappointing (*"We still need to develop the business, sir, you have to understand."*), next to the prince hardly anybody speaks English

Distributorships are like mushrooms. You find out too late whether they are good or bad.

– based on a Woody Allen quote on marriage

(*"No problem, I will be happy to translate your emails to my people."*), they are mainly strong in Ankara but absolutely not present in Istanbul and Izmir (*"We know, sir, but we are working on that."*) and they are not present in some of the segments that you want to target, although the website did show products in that area (*"That is a very small market only in Turkey but we plan to hire somebody for that very soon."*). Unfortunately, I have to refer to the dog whisperer, Cesar Millan, again. The problem is not the distributor (the dog). It is you, the leader of the pack that made a mistake. Your homework was not done properly.

Do your homework in advance, be pro-active, use a checklist (which I will share later) and go find distributors yourself, rather than being found by them. Identifying more and better distributors is a continuous mission, even if today you are happy with the ones you have. Know what you want to achieve and in which other market segments you want to be or become active. Decide whether you can do a better job yourself or whether you will need business partners to achieve your goal. Next, which type of partners do you need to achieve this goal? Fail to do your homework and you will walk into the "trap of opportunism". You are also doomed to give too much away too fast to your new Prince Charming.

All my contacts with companies confirm how few companies really take the time to define in writing the profile of their ideal business partners. Because of this, ANY company presenting itself to you and operating in your virgin territory COULD indeed be the right one. *We have nothing to lose,* is often the reaction you will hear from managers. Well, think again, there is a lot to lose if you fail to make the right choice. Your distributors are your representation, defending your company flag and your image in that market. Make a mistake and your business, as well as your reputation, will suffer. Unfortunately, hoping for the best is not a strategy.

Hope is not a strategy.
– Rudy Giuliani

So how do you best proceed in identifying a good partner? I try to break the evaluation down into what I like to refer to as the **3 Cs**.

> **Capability (can they?)**
> **Compliance (will they?)**
> **Commitment (do they want to?)**

Is the distributor capable of doing what you expect them to do? Is there enough indication that they also will do what you expect from them? And finally, do you see the necessary drive, motivation, hunger to work really hard for you or are you merely going to be there to make them look good?

Capability (can they?)

Love is blind, also when it comes to choosing your distributors. Visually attractive company presentations, ambitious statements by Prince General Manager and your drive to finally beat that one competitor, all of the above can be reasons to jump to conclusions on your future business partner. But, a distributorship is not a one-night stand. A distributorship is a marriage, also maybe not for eternity anymore like before, but still a marriage. Even without a marriage contract (distributor agreement), it is serious business.

I am aware that checking out your future bride or groom from head to toe – the whole distributor history, the whole organization – is still no 100% guarantee for knowing all about your partner and also no guarantee for eternal love. But, I believe that my checklist below can potentially lead to an at least more satisfactory business life together.

Let us address the first question: CAN they be the partner that you expect, CAN they meet your expectations?

Topic	Examples
Coverage	» In which markets and market segments is the distributor active? » In which demographic target segments is the distributor active? » In which geographical area is the physical presence of the distributor stronger/weaker? (check e.g. customer installed base) » How does annual revenue break down between public (e.g. tenders) and private market?
Market intimacy (knowledge)	» How well does the distributor know his target customers, decision makers? (how/why?) » Which of the current distributor activities give access to the same target audience as yours? » Which are your future direct competitors and how much valuable information does the distributor own?
Reputation	» What is the general market perception about the distributor? (seek input at customer events, tradeshows, field visits) » Are they purely price oriented or rather premium quality and customer service focused? » Has there been a lot of staff turnover in past years? » How do other, non-competing vendors enjoy working with the same distributor? » Which key customers are part of their customer base?
Organization	» What is the size of their team (sales, marketing, support)? » How many of these people and who will really be working for your products and services? » For which other products, activities are those same people responsible?
Skills	» What is the background, work history of the team? » What is their experience related to your target segments? » Do they have the technical skills required to represent and support your products? » Are the language skills in place to communicate efficiently with your team?

Financial	» What is the revenue and profit evolution of the company? » What will be the share of your business segment in their total revenue? » What is their estimated cash flow situation?

Probably none of your potential distributors will score to perfection on each of the questions that you come up with. But this is where your expertise as the account manager or general manager comes in. It is your role to make an estimate of how much progress is possible in each of the areas that are the most critical to you and how much time this may cost.

Compliance (will they?)

I believe that it is vital to initiate the discussion upfront with your potential distributor on the weaknesses that were identified in your capability test and to seek formal commitment on how they will close the gaps. *"We will definitely look into that"*, *"We plan to hire somebody for that segment down the road"*, unfortunately may be just too open-ended. Request deadlines and potentially even include them in the enclosures to your distributor agreement. Also product training at your facilities within a reasonable time prior or just after the start of the agreement may be another perfect example of a formal commitment that is required.

Even if the distributor seems to be able to do what you expect, then this is no guarantee that it will happen. WILL they immediately press the accelerator for you? Sometimes it is written in the stars that distributors will "take" your products in their bag but they will not really promote them. Unfortunately, your product is often simply "interesting" to add to the portfolio, but in reality it may not immediately be a priority for the distributor to also sell intensively. Call it "window dressing", with which your distributor can present himself more strongly in the market as, for example, the one stop shop for each end-customer.

In practice, however, you have now handed over your sales position to a distributor and the customer may still be pushed by them in the direction of other technological solutions or even competing products. This can happen because, for example, those other products provide higher product margins, are less complex to sell, get better vendor support, or simply require less effort for the same financial result. In addition to a nicer display case, the distributor has immediately reduced a lot of competition – namely, yours. And if you don't pay attention, you'll just walk into the trap.

Here too, a small checklist and pro-active questioning can save you from a few basic mistakes, or at least strongly reduce the risk. Check out these example questions.

Topic	Examples
Strategy	» What strategy does the company generally carry out? » What strategic objectives have they formulated for your segment? » How does your solution, your portfolio fit in their strategy? » Why do they want to offer your solutions, your portfolio?
Business plan	» How are they going to commercialize your products and solutions? » What does their detailed sales activity plan look like? » Which profit margins do they wish to apply to your products?
Portfolio	» Which product groups and brands do they carry? » Is their offer sufficiently selective or do they want to be the big supermarket where you can get just about everything? » Do they offer competing products and does this constitute a problem for you?

Various conversations with more than just one employee at the potential or existing distributor will often already do the job. It can immediately show you how important you really are to them today or will be later. We will refer to this in a next chapter with the beautiful terminology of "share of mind". During the ever-important visit to the offices of a new distributor, I always ask for a quick tour through the warehouse. Try to see with your own eyes which products mainly take up the warehouse space and the most activity. The unsuspecting warehouse manager will proudly tell and show it all to you. Let me put it like this: "What fills the heart does fill the warehouse". And finally, the distributor's showroom can provide also confirmation, but it may also be rearranged just before your visit, so no real guarantee. These are no fairy tales. I have seen it all happen with my own eyes.

Commitment (want they?)

With the word "WANT" I refer to the feeling of hunger that your existing or potential distributors must show. Call it fighting spirit if you want, which for me is just that little bit more than "agreeing" to work with you. A nice quote says: "It is not about the size of the dog in the fight, it's about the size of the fight in the dog." (Mark Twain) Not the size of your distributor is important but especially how hard he is willing to fight for you later, that is what really counts.

What the correct size of a distributor should be, is maybe difficult to determine, but I like to define it as follows: if your distributor would lose the distributorship for your portfolio again later for whatever reason, then a business pain must arise at that distributor. This way you increase the chance that he will "want" to work for you. If this pain would be completely absent due to the many alternatives that are available to them, or due to too small a share of your portfolio in the turnover and margin of the distributor, then it is only to wait and see if they will really work very hard for you. We will discuss how you can and why you should stimulate this "share of mind" in a later chapter.

Of course, the "WANT" also applies to your side. I remember plenty of my own sales contacts where the potential distributor revealed information that deprived me of the will to cooperate. If, for example, you hear from the 63-year-old manager that he is disappointed that his son does not want to take over his one-man company within two years, then your will to go with this partner may be rather limited. You are looking for an ambitious and long term partner, not one that is perfectly happy with the current business and plans to retire with no succession in two years from now.

Most people fail, not because of lack of desire, but because of lack of commitment.

– Vince Lombardi

Finding Nemo

If you have already taken the time needed to determine what the ideal distributor looks like and if you have also become aware of the opportunism trap, then for many the question still remains: how and where do I find potential distributors at all? How do I proceed especially in a country that I know less well today? There are many roads that lead to Rome and unfortunately some of those roads are underused by companies. I would like to sum up some options for you, however not necessarily in order of the expected success.

» Investment & Trade Associations
  (e.g. Flanders Investment & Trade in my region)
» Chamber of Commerce
» Embassies
» LinkedIn
» Google
» Suppliers
» Network
» Trade fairs

For Belgian (Flemish) readers amongst you, Flanders Investment & Trade is organized regionally and also has representatives abroad. They can give concrete answers to your questions, including distributor profiles, and they make suggestions about potential distribution channels if you want them to. The Chamber of Commerce (VoKa in Flanders) is also regionally organized and also carries a database (Kompass) that can help you draw up a shortlist of potential distributors. The focus of VoKa is – in my experience – more on helping companies through training (how to do business with…).

LinkedIn is also a good basis for your search, because – in addition to finding companies in this social network – you can immediately view the profiles of the employees of the company through appropriate filtering. How long have they been with the company? What is their background? Are they sufficiently familiar with your target group? An even broader search can always be done via Google and other browsers.

Make sure to consult websites of other manufacturers and suppliers to your target group. View the distributors with whom they have started working in that one country that you are exploring. Ask those suppliers also directly about the performance of their distributor. But keep in mind that not everyone is eager to share his partner with you soon. The names of these distributors also help trade associations and Chamber of Commerce in understanding better the type of distributors you want.

Also ask as many end-customers as possible that you meet at a trade fair or other customer event. Who is their supplier today? What are their experiences with their own suppliers and do they know other ones? And finally, do not forget to consult your own professional network.

In summary, with a "distributors wanted" sign on your trade fair booth, you will almost certainly attract the wrong distributors, so I personally do not recommend this route. From now on, make sure you take the time to pre-determine the profile of the ideal distributor. Also use it as a guide for improving your current distributors. Make sure you are looking for distributors yourself instead of being found. Ask the right questions before you sign up for marriage and explore all available resources in your search for that Prince or Princess Charming.

Signing stronger distributor agreements

You have identified a new distributor that meets enough of your expectations. You are ready to start doing business with them. You do have distributor agreements already in place with existing business partners but you may want to critically review those as well at this point. Let's see how we can build a solid template for your future distributor agreements and how we can improve the ones you currently have in place and may be up for renewal.

TO CONTRACT OR NOT TO CONTRACT

That indeed is the question. Opinions differ among business people whether you should or should not have written agreements in place with your distributors. On this matter I can only share my personal opinion and mine is clearly... yes! Why? This is because contracts are not made in the first place for the good days. Rather it is meant to help you in resolving discussions at times where things get out of control, at times where parties seem to disagree on the initial intentions or execution of their partnership.

The issue with distributor agreements is that they are established at a time when usually nothing but mutual euphoria exists about the partners and their partnership. There is a high level of mutual trust, both parties are very ambitious and believe that together they will conquer the world, or at least a small part of it. Reality strikes sometimes already just a few months later.

I was ruined twice,
once when I lost a lawsuit,
once when I won one.

– Voltaire

Having the most relevant topics written down in a formal distributor agreement, will take the partnership beyond a trial-and-error status. It will also reduce the risk of getting into expensive lawsuits that could have been avoided if parties had been more explicit on day one about what they actually agreed and the mutual expectations.

Many mistakes are made when drawing up distributor agreements, most of which I will try to cover in this chapter. What I have decided not to include in this book are contract templates. One reason is because I am not a legal expert, and secondly because good contract templates may simply differ strongly by industry. So my general recommendation is to try and get copies, examples of similar contracts to the one you are trying to draw up from within your own industry. Check them out and see how you can make yours even better. This is next to my recommendations below.

EXCLUSIVE OR NON-EXCLUSIVE

I like to address this issue of exclusivity separately because it usually arises at an early stage in your contract negotiations. Distributors generally request this by default and do so for obvious reasons. However, I believe you should not grant exclusivity, definitely not at the beginning of the partnership, and even only in exceptional cases later on. I will share with you why.

The main reason that distributors firmly request exclusivity is because you're their new vendor and they don't know you yet. Are you a trustworthy vendor that will stick to his commitments? Are you not going to take over once they have developed the market for you? Will their playground be large enough and long enough in time to have return on their initial investment? Distributors dislike building a market presence for you and then see you run off with another partner that can capitalize on the foundation that they have created for you and them. Their initial investments may include a showroom, warehouse space, staff training, presence at multiple trade fairs, advertising in industry magazines and much more.

However, the opposite is true as well. The distributor is also new to you. If you agree to exclusivity from day one and sign a contract for a period of minimum three years (which is often what distributors will request at the start), then any failure to choose the right distributor may lock you out for several years from a promising market or segment. Why would you?

What always worked for me as a compromise solution is making contracts for a one-year-period (two years at best) with silent renewals three months prior to the termination date and with a gentlemen's agreement that you will not initiate any other partnership in the assigned region as long as the financial targets in the agreement are met. The importance of setting financial targets with regular measurement points will be covered later. And here the importance of having a clear strategy in place for the region involved also becomes eminent already. If you are not clear on the journey, how can you ever draw up agreements that make sense?

I will come back to standard mistakes that are often being made in distributor agreements, but you will have only one shot at the initial "exclusive or non-exclusive" option. Granting it from day one will give you a much harder time later on when you decide that you want to step out of the agreement again or want to appoint additional distributors.

ATTORNEYS ARE NOT BUSINESS PEOPLE

I am the last person to doubt the importance of attorneys in drawing up a good distributor agreement. I think you must involve experts in building your contract template. Also, they play a major role in case of conflict situations and in avoiding or managing lawsuits. However, I always like to break the agreement down into two major parts:

» The legal part (fixed)
» The business part (variable)

Preferably the distributor agreement consists of a **legal** part which is fixed and should not be touched anymore afterwards. This part should cover all of the standard paragraphs and clauses that a good industry distributor agreement should hold, including the parties that sign the agreement, definitions and terminology used, subject of the agreement, the initial contract duration, ordering, delivery and payment procedures, notification periods on topics like price changes, contract termination or extension and product changes. It best also includes clauses on warranty, regulatory affairs, changes of ownership, liabilities, place of jurisdiction and alike. And of course it will be sealed with the signature of both parties.

Anything related to **business** is however covered by preference in the enclosures and should be referred to in the legal part of the agreement. These enclosures are what I would call the "variable part of the agreement". This section will hold details like the sales region, the portfolio that the distributor will be allowed to sell, the pricing and alike.

Advantage of respecting these two building blocks in an agreement is that you should not read the legal part again and again, in case of discussions and you won't be faced with any surprises five or ten years later because something valuable was modified just that one time for that one distributor. The legal section should be fixed, approved by an attorney and known to the whole organization. The variable business part on the other hand gives your sales management the advantage that changes in pricing, portfolio, region or whatever else you have just agreed to change, does not require a review of the whole agreement but just requires changing or adding one little addendum to the agreement. Sign this one and you're done.

In summary

» Let the attorneys work on the legal part but keep control over the business part, whatever the size of your company and business.
» However, involve your attorneys in the daily business. Bring them into the game, also when things are going well, so they better understand your business proposals or decisions. As I will mention elsewhere in this book, companies do not do business, people do. Get your attorneys also emotionally involved in your business and you will have good partners when you need them at your side.
» Try to avoid that your attorneys present thirty pages agreements to you and your distributors. They scare off your potential distributors and usually have no added value. Force your attorneys to be concise and to limit themselves to the essence of the agreement. The distributors will show higher trust in you.

KEY "BUSINESS" TOPICS IN AGREEMENTS

Since I do not have a legal background, I will limit myself in this book to what I believe to be the twenty most essential topics from a business perspective that should best be included in a distributor agreement if possible. They are not ranked in order of importance but should rather act as an inspiration to you.

Top 20 Business Topics in Distributor Agreements

» Territory
  - Description of the contracted region
» Portfolio
  - Detailed description of the contracted portfolio (product names)
» Channels
  - Description of already existing channels in the territory
  - Existence of a vendor web shop as alternative channel
  - Distributor's obligation to report and get formal approval from vendor on the appointment of sub-distributors
» Exclusivity
  - (Non)-exclusivity from vendor towards distributor (competing distributors)
  - (Non)-exclusivity from distributor towards vendor (competing products)
» Sales lead management
  - Sales leads handling from trade fairs, vendor website and alike
» End-user access
  - Accountability to give vendor access to end-user information or end-user contact when requested
» Pricing
  - Standard product pricing (applicable pricelist)
  - Availability and conditions for demo products
  - Demo or new launches pricing
  - Special pricing programs
  - Price changes and change notification period
  - Currency deviations
  - Accountability on duties, customs, taxes

- » Delivery
  - ▪ Responsibility for product acceptance
  - ▪ Accountability in case of delayed deliveries
- » Payment
  - ▪ Payment terms and conditions
- » Overdue Payment
  - ▪ Charges for overdue payments (best include even if never applied by you in reality)
- » License agreement
  - ▪ End-user license agreement
- » Purchase orders
  - ▪ Order process
  - ▪ Procedures in case of order cancellation
- » Order volume
  - ▪ Quarterly and/or annual purchase targets
  - ▪ Possible incentives in case of target achievement
  - ▪ Impact/penalties in case of underperformance
- » Order forecast
  - ▪ Forecasting frequency
  - ▪ Binding character of the distributor forecast
- » Services
  - ▪ Required service capabilities of the distributor
  - ▪ Inventory
  - ▪ Requirements regarding storage infrastructure for your products
  - ▪ Inventory rotation guidelines
  - ▪ Product return procedures
  - ▪ Product discontinuation procedures
- » Training
  - ▪ Obligations regarding vendor training participation
  - ▪ Obligations of end-user training by the distributor
- » Communication
  - ▪ Vendor corporate guidelines (reference can be made to a corporate identity handbook if existing)
  - ▪ Listing on mutual websites
  - ▪ General rules on marketing development funding
  - ▪ Advertising/Social Media/...

» Contract duration
  - Notification period (if not already included in the legal part)
  - Standard extension period in case of renewal
» Contract termination
  - List of possible reasons for termination
  - Post-termination remaining obligations for both parties

THE MOST COMMON AGREEMENT MISTAKES

When reviewing or discussing distributor agreements with companies, I have come across standard mistakes or what I would call at least missed opportunities. Let me share with you the ten most common ones. Some have already briefly been mentioned above. Again, the list is non-exhaustive but can hopefully inspire you to also critically review your existing agreements and draw up better ones for the future or at the renewal date.

Top 10 Distributor Agreement Mistakes

1	Exclusivity
2	Giving away too much, too fast
3	No annual or semi-automatic renewal
4	Frequency of amendments
5	Frequency of price changes
6	Termination by one party only
7	Termination for cause only
8	What happens after termination
9	No comparison with proven industry agreements
10	Leaving the contract negotiations to attorneys

» **Exclusivity** was covered above, but I stated there that exceptions may exist where exclusivity could make sense indeed. One of them is that countries or potential market segments may just be too small for multiple players to act. Another one could be that the start-up investment for a distributor is exceptionally high and the return on investment needs protection.

Non-exclusivity however holds many advantages for you, including having a backup in case one distributor fails to perform and whose contract maybe even needs to be terminated. More sources of market information are available to you. There exists some level of healthy competition this way and not every distributor has the same customer contacts and expertise. In the end, it will be your business judgement what makes most sense to your company and to your market.

» **Giving away too much, too fast**. This is probably the most common mistake in distributor agreements. A whole country and the whole vendor's portfolio are many times included in the initial contract. Again, this is because contracts are made at a time of euphoria on the one hand and because distributors demand it most of the time.

However, just like with exclusivity the reality is that distributors are not equally strong in all regions of the country. Their customer base is generally not well spread over your target segments. Failing to define your strategy and to do the necessary market research will lead too often to you just agreeing to the whole country and to the whole portfolio from day one. I call it "the road of the least resistance", which is one that you may regret at a later stage.

My recommendation is to start with a region, large or small, in line with their geographical presence and only giving access to the products in your portfolio that answer to the needs of the specific customer segments in which the distributor has a proven presence, has a customer base and holds valuable contacts. Everything else can be added easily at any time after proof of success and commitment to your brand.

» **No annual or semi-automatic renewal**. Making the agreement renewable on an annual base will keep the pressure high on your distributor and in most cases will lead to higher performance. Later in this book we will refer to it as creating and keeping "share of mind".

In case of underperformance, my recommendations regarding target setting, distributor evaluation and coaching can be implemented more easily. We will discuss this later. This way you avoid too long delays in getting your distributor back on track. Many companies suffer from procrastination when it comes to taking the more difficult and invasive decision that the partnership would better be terminated.

» **Frequency of amendments**. Too often contracts mention that amendments can be made only once a year. Although the purpose cannot be to do so continuously, I believe amendments to the agreement should be possible at any time. This can sometimes even be to the benefit of both parties.

» **Frequency of price changes**. The same applies here. Although it is understandable that distributors want to secure their margins, that they want to be able to send out price quotes to end-customers with guaranteed pricing for a certain period, a reasonable notification period for price changes should allow you to change prices at any time when needed. The reasons for this of course may differ strongly by industry and can for instance be driven by raw material cost prices.

Commitments made by distributors to end-users are often used as a reason why they cannot accept your next price increase. But if they haven't consulted you on any specific longer term project, you are not responsible for commitments made by your distributor. It is just another good reason for me to have distributor agreements in place and to avoid unnecessary discussions when such things happen.

» **Termination by one party only**. To the advantage of the distributors, my recommendation is that distributor agreements should be cancellable by both parties, not only by the vendor, as you may find in some agreements. The simple reason is that one-directional cancellation is doomed to lead to legal disputes and lawsuits, initiated by the distributor and, whatever the outcome, never turning you into a winner. It will hurt your image in the market and potentially cost you a fortune.

A bad agreement is better than a good lawsuit.

– Italian proverb

» **Termination for cause only**. I see no need to include a truly restrictive list of potential causes in your agreement – like you will typically see only bankruptcy, change of ownership or other specific causes mentioned. No cause at all or just convenience should be a good enough reason to separate. If for whatever reason the collaboration does no longer make sense, parties should be able to terminate it. My experience in the medical imaging field holds examples where traditional medical film distributors were just not the right partners in the evolving digital imaging software world. A change in the market reality should be enough reason to go out and identify other parties when the existing ones are not willing to evolve.

» **What happens after termination?** It may sound weird to already be thinking about how to potentially split your belongings in case of a separation on your wedding day. Unfortunately, agreements are not made in the first place for the good days but for the days when things can possibly start to go wrong. Therefore it is good to think about and put down in writing upfront what should happen in case of a separation. What about the pending orders? What about inventory still in the distributor warehouse? How about mandatory service to the existing customer base and parts inventory? Which rules apply during the notification period and which ones after the full termination?

Contract termination is usually a process that damages both parties. The more you can reduce that risk in your initial agreement, the better. But only few divorces take place in a friendly and supportive way. Mud and dirt may be flying around your head, so why not cover yourself as best as possible?

» **No comparison with proven industry agreements**. Unfortunately, too many of us believe that we can make contracts ourselves by doing some copy-paste of templates on the Internet. I have already given my advice on the use of attorneys but also want to recommend you to cross-check with agreements that you can get hold of from within the industry. These can be agreements from the competition but also those from other suppliers to the same distributor.

» **Leaving the contract negotiations to attorneys**. Beware of legal departments that sometimes feel the need to make extensive agreements to underline the importance of their role within the company. It usually leads to a lot of frustration within the sales and marketing department and to lack of trust on the side of the distributor. Overacting by corporate counsels on the legal side may jeopardize the business side of the partnership.

4

MANAGING YOUR DISTRIBUTORS

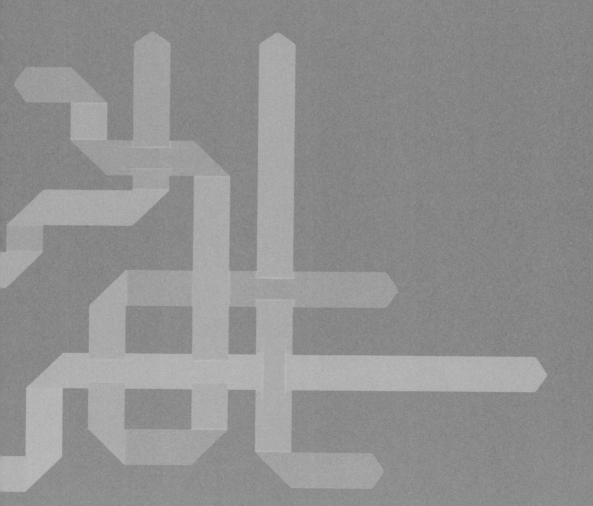

Many companies believe to have a clear and strong value proposition to their end-users. However, when asked about it, the best that usually comes to the table are common buzzwords like best quality, service, support or training. Exceptionally, companies may indeed have a clear and strong end-user value proposition. Seldom however do companies spend time thinking about their value proposition to the distributors.

Next to being an "extension" of your own organization, we also defined distributors earlier as being your "customers". So why would they not be entitled to a clear value proposition as well? What sets you apart from the other vendors that sell to them, even when no direct competition to you? Why should they work hard for you if your company offering to them, at least in their perception, is no more than just standard? From here on you need to start thinking outside of your products and focus on identifying what you offer that makes the tasks of your distributors more efficient and successful. What helps them sell your products with the highest possible hit rate and profit margin?

In this chapter I will help you understand why customers (don't) buy from you. I will take you through the basics of value based selling. I will educate you on how to develop the listening skills that are needed for successful value selling and how to implement all of this in working with your distributors.

Why customers (don't) buy from you

I always ask my trainees at the start of a session why they believe that customers do or should buy from their company. Almost without any exception these are the predictable answers I get:

>> quality of our products
>> completeness of our portfolio
>> our customer support
>> our technical service
>> our customer training
>> we have the best value for money

Interesting. This is exactly what each of the participants believes to be the reasons customers should choose their company. And even more interesting, when checking out the competition websites, their sales arguments do not seem to differ from yours. So it is literally nothing more than the Olympic minimum, needed to participate in the Olympic Games. But it is not going to win you a medal.

Other reasons, other decision parameters apparently play a part when customers decided to buy from you or decided not to. It also means – and this is the good news – that a different approach, another way of working than the standard arguments, can truly set you apart from your direct competition. Let them continue doing what they're used to, that's fine. Let me take you one step back here and ask you a very basic question: what is sales, in fact?

What is sales?

It may sound as a strange question to you, sales or marketing professionals, and most of you will probably respond with the most common definition you can think of, like this standard definition from the Internet: "Sales is the activity or business of selling products and services" (www.businessdictionary.com).

Although technically correct, I would like to suggest a switch to one that defines sales as "helping a customer in taking a buying decision". This little twist puts the customer more in the centre and will help you, later on in this chapter, to better understand the importance of value based selling and why customers buy or do not buy from you.

Sales is helping a customer in taking a buying decision.

Let us start with a very simple exercise to get to my point. What do you see here? (Please answer spontaneously before continuing.)

Some of you may say it is the letter B, others may say it is the number 13. Here's how I will slightly mislead my trainees whenever I ask them the same question. Half of the participants are shown this picture first:

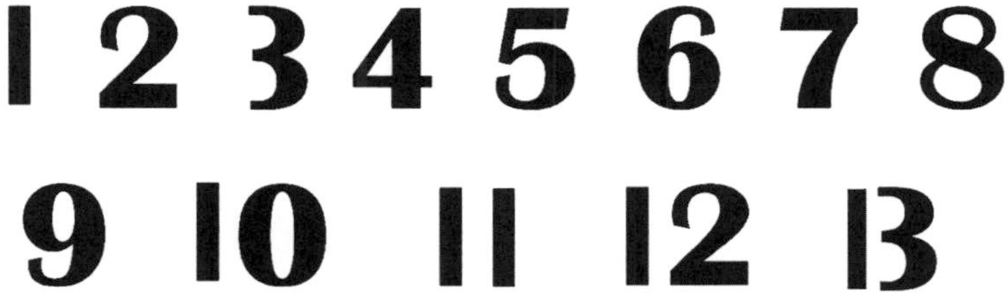

1 2 3 4 5 6 7 8
9 10 11 12 13

The other half of the group gets to see this:

A B C D E F
G H I J K L

Then they are shown the B or 13 and their statement will no doubt be influenced by what they saw earlier. They are all looking at the same symbol but they read it differently, due to the context. Let's call it their previous experience or the expectation that I created. I managed to influence their answer in a fairly simple way.

Let's do another quick exercise. How many squares can you identify in the following figure? Again, be a good sport and spend a few seconds looking at the figure before continuing.

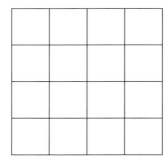

First of all, every group will have that one Einstein amongst them that will say: "None, sir, since you cannot guarantee that they still are squares when projected with a beamer". It makes sense. The correct answer is 30 squares. And since – like most of your peers – you may have counted too few, I will first and quickly give you the why of the 30 squares:

16 x single squares
9 x 2 by 2 squares
4 x 3 by 3 squares
1 x 4 by 4 square
———————————
= 30 squares total

If your answer was correct, then you are not a value based selling expert yet! This little test is not meant as an IQ or sales skills test. It only helps you understand that although we were all looking at exactly the same picture, a very simple, tangible one, we still had a different "perception" of what we were seeing.

And the keyword is out... PERCEPTION.

Customers buy based on perception

The reason customers buy or don't buy from you is all because of perception. You may have the proven best quality, the best service, the best support team and training courses, but if that one customer in front of you does not see it or does not perceive it as such, the value that you offer is perceived as less by that one particular customer. The perceived value will be lower than what you believe it to be.

Mind the key words in that last but one sentence. It states "... by that particular customer". Indeed, perception is not general for the whole market. It is different for each customer. Even if the entire sales team states continuously that you are too expensive, still hundreds of customers decided to buy from you in the past years. And they did so for a reason. So why is that? It is because they individually perceived that the value of your offer

The reason customers buy from you is perception.

exceeded the cost (price or other) to acquire those products or services from you. As we will discuss later, there may have been competition at play but potentially also none at all. They wanted to buy from you, or rather from your distributor, for a reason.

If you would go to a U2 concert and would select just ten people at the exit that all cry out loud that the concert was "amazing", would they all give the same reasons for it, you think? No, they wouldn't. However, they all witnessed the same live performance. They all heard the same quality of voices and sound, through the same loudspeakers. Some however may have enjoyed the light show, the huge video screens and the atmosphere most. Others may have loved the classics in the band's playlist. Still others may have been flabbergasted by the exceptional guitar play of their hero David Evans (nicknamed "The Edge"). One younger visitor may have perceived it as amazing just because this was his very first visit ever to a rock concert and he enjoyed the company of his new girlfriend.

Perception is not just individual. It can also be influenced. I remember an experiment with a game of soccer that was shown in two separate rooms. It was exactly the same game, at the same time, to two different audiences, but commented by two different sports reporters. One was highlighting the positive of the home team throughout the entire game while in the other room the commentator was focusing on the negative. When asked at the end of the game how well they thought the team performed, guess what the general perception was? Exactly! Their perception was completely influenced by the reporter (as happens to us over and over again when we are watching the news, reading magazines or checking out our friend's Facebook pages).

This is all great news for us, business people. We do understand that customers buy from us based on perception. And so do your distributors. It is an individual thing and it can also be influenced. You don't have to be the best at everything in order to sell. You should try to excel in what really matters to your customers!

There are things known and there are things unknown, and in between are the doors of perception.
– Aldous Huxley

So let us stop repeating over and over again at our internal sales meetings that we are too expensive, that our competition is better known in the market, that we offer too low quality compared to the number one in the market, or whatever excuse we may still have for our underperformance. Let us rather work on understanding why so many distributors and customers *do* buy from us. And try to find ways to further improve that customer perception. Try to identify what adds value to your individual customers and to your distributors. That's what value based selling is about.

The buying decision – when perceived value exceeds cost

I stated that sales could best be defined as "helping customers in taking a buying decision". So when will customers actually buy then? When the balance between the "perceived" value and the cost to acquire it is positive, the balance can potentially flip from a non-buying to a buying decision. In general the "cost to acquire it" is assumed to be the price, but it is definitely not the only cost.

Customers buy when the perceived value exceeds the cost to acquire it.

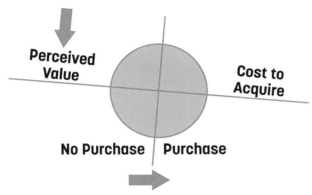

How companies influence perception

Successful companies have different strategies and different ways – but usually also hugely different budgets – to work on that customer perception. Would you agree that Microsoft Office and Mercedes are two popular brands that try to create the perception of offering very reliable products? Would you not perceive Tesla as a more innovative type of company? You definitely know Red Bull but you probably don't know anything about the ingredients of their product. This is because you can create and influence perception at different levels and in different ways, some of which require massive marketing budgets that most of us simply do not have.

The levels at which value perception can be created, are nicely summarized in what literature calls the "Total Value Experience" and is often presented as different layers in the "onion model" below. Each of the levels can create and influence perceived value.

Microsoft Office, Mercedes and many other established quality brands of this world focus mainly on creating value perception in the centre of the onion model, on the product level itself. Tesla or Pfizer – the latter invented Viagra – are examples of companies that have managed to create value perception mainly through innovation. When asking people outside of the pharma industry, only few will be able to mention many other Pfizer products or activities.

Red Bull and Apple are two example companies that almost exclusively work on the branding layer in the onion. Red Bull management openly claims that they do not really sell their product, they only do marketing. By investing highly in extreme sports they create the perception that Red Bull takes you to a performance level that you believed impossible till then. It gives you wings.

Unfortunately, most companies depend on the sales and services layer to create the value perception for end-users and distributors, yours probably too. This is the outer layer of the onion and the reason why the basics of value based selling matter so much to you and to your team. Value based selling should also matter to your distributors because their sales and service activities are usually the only significant tools they have available to create perceived value. They generally need your help and support in that area and many companies fail to deliver that. As you will learn, there are many ways you can help them and create a higher share of mind. Start to communicate in a different way about your products, train your own staff and then train your distributors. It will help you in making their task easier, in getting more share of mind and in having the distributors work harder for you.

Who are your "customers"?

For some managers it is already a challenge to build a value proposition for their products or solutions. Some indeed have difficulties expressing which customer it needs to respond to. They know perfectly well what their product does, but are not always clear in describing the value it adds to the customer. In the best-case scenario, the focus will be on the end-user value proposition only. And even then, sometimes more with a vendor-centric focus than with a customer-centric focus.

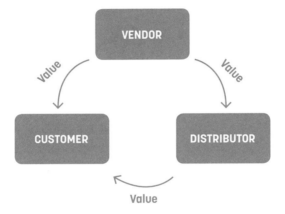

Value can and should be created at three levels. This is where it becomes obvious again – as mentioned a few times now – that distributors should be looked at through two different lenses. They are a customer but also an extension of your organization. Or, another way to put it:

> In business to distributors
> you are selling TO them and
> THROUGH them.

Neglect one of the three value creation chains and your total result will be affected. All three interactions matter in trying to maximize the perceived value to the end-customers. Understanding these three levels and working on each of them specifically in the future will lead to an increased total value experience by your end-customers, leading to increased and more profitable sales to both you and your distributors. And they will like you for that and reward you with more share of mind.

But getting more out of your distributors clearly starts again with you, the vendor! In the next chapter I will suggest a logical approach to work on the value propositions to your end-customers and to your distributors.

The basics of value based selling

WHY VALUE OUTWEIGHS UNIQUENESS

When kicking off a training session on value based selling, I always like to start with a simple story: the Umbrella Story. I split the trainees into two groups and then I go tell them each a different story.

Group 1 are told that we are at a funeral. It starts to rain unexpectedly. Nobody brought an umbrella but fortunately a little stall nearby is selling umbrellas. The retail price is five euros and the cost price to the vendor is two euros. After having sold all black umbrellas – an obvious choice at a funeral – the only one left is a bright yellow version with Disney characters on it. So not exactly suited for the occasion. So the vendor is forced to lower his price on that yellow one if he still wants to sell it at this funeral. You are the vendor. What is the lowest price you would sell it for?

Group 2 are told that they are working as a tour guide, taking thirty Chinese tourists around the city of Brussels. It starts to rain and again, no one brought an umbrella (though it seems to rain a lot in Belgium, doesn't it?). All the tourists quickly run to the stall to go and buy umbrellas. But, you as the tour guide want to stand out in the crowd and therefore you run to get your umbrella first. You want a shiny one. There is only one bright yellow umbrella with Disney characters between all the black ones, which will definitely do the job for you. But, the yellow one is more expensive. How much would you, the tourist guide, be willing to pay more for this yellow one if the standard black ones cost five euros?

We are talking about the same yellow umbrella in both stories, with the same cost price to the vendor. The Group 1 vendors usually agree to sell at around three euros and like to still make a little profit. The Group 2 tourist guides usually agree to spend up to eight euros or even slightly more on their unique yellow one. Why is that? Because the perceived value of the yellow umbrella with Disney characters is completely different in both stories.

Only sales people who understand the difference in value to their customers will be able to maximize their sales prices. Average sales people will be happy with the margin they still make with their three euros sales price ("That's still a good margin, boss!"). Your greatest sales people are the ones that understand the value of your offering to each of your individual customers and are able to convey it also properly to each of them, over and over again. They are not taking, what I already referred to as "the road of the least resistance".

Great sales people are value experts.

STOP SELLING. START LISTENING

But how can you find out what the value is to each of your customers? In the umbrella story it was maybe obvious for the two different vendors what the value was going to be in each of the two cases. They both would not need to ask a lot of questions because the value immediately could have been very clear to them. In reality, the process of finding out what does and what does not add value to this one specific customer in front of you, is a much more complex story.

Many of us, sales people, claim – even with some arrogance – that we are great at one thing... listening to our distributors! However, nothing is further from the truth. Next time you are at a tradeshow with your team, listen to the conversations taking place between account managers and distributors. After having asked a few standard questions on how their business is doing, whether George from Region South is doing better now and whether this one deal with the London authorities did materialize in the end, ninety percent of the time WE do the talking. WE explain all the great features of our newest product line. WE stress how well our company is doing. WE have a special launch promotion for the distributor on the new model there in the centre of the booth. WE proudly show our updated, glossy product brochures and WE give the distributor an exclusive invitation for the international distributor event tomorrow evening.

At best we may spend ten percent of the time asking really relevant questions that help us understand the true value of our offering to that specific distributor. Why should we? We believe to know them already, since we have been working with them for so many years. You may disagree, but trust me, not many sales talks are different from the one above. When deals do not materialize, if competition takes over, we so often claim that it was because of price. That is what made the difference. The truth is often that we just forgot to evaluate what was adding value for this one customer. We assumed to know but we never asked.

So there's only one clear message:

> Stop selling. Start listening.

Let me repeat this for those of you who weren't paying attention...

> # Stop selling. Start listening.

Reverse the ninety percent talking to ninety percent listening and only then you will be able to find out what has value to your customer. This applies to the interaction between you and your distributors, as well as to the interaction between your distributors and their end-customers.

THE SPIN LISTENING METHOD

Learning to listen is easier said than done. How can we get better at listening to our distributors and end-customers? How can we find out fastest what has value to our distributor or end-customer? What is our customer willing to pay a premium price for? And what may have no value to him or her at all? We may believe to have a truly unique value offering, but does this one specific customer feel the same?

In literature you can find several suggested techniques. The one that works best for me is one that I learned through a funny sales training video from

British actor John Cleese. The approach was simple and effective. Here is a summary for you.

SPIN is short for the consecutive questions that you should prepare, practice and raise in chronological order during your customer sales meetings. The answers and what you do with them, lead to a very strong and customized value proposition, applicable to that one single and specific customer:

Situational questions

Problem questions

Implementation questions

Needs statement

The basic idea is the following. When meeting with potential customers, you don't and should not have hours to waste. Usually you will only get a few minutes. In the best-case scenario, you have a few hours or so to really talk business. That precious time should not be lost on you trying to run at Usain-Bolt-speed through all the features and benefits that marketing has identified on your portfolio. You should not hope and expect that in the middle of this information hurricane, one or two relevant topics will potentially hit the brain of your customer, stay there and automatically be translated into a buying decision. It is not going to happen.

Less is more. You should primarily focus on what is relevant to your customer's value creation. Remember the drawing of that balance, where you were looking for extra weight on the left-hand side (value perception) in order to outweigh the cost to acquire it (including price) on the right-hand side.

One golden rule: all your questions should be "open" questions. This means only questions to which the answer cannot just be "yes" or "no". Closed questions bring little information and generally are a waste of time. The purpose of open questions is that the customer speaks, not you. Also learn to use the power of silence. Do not immediately respond after the customer stops talking. Keep quiet and they will give you even more valuable information. But most important, try to keep your mouth shut. And yes, I plead guilty too, trust me.

I will limit my example questions below to the interaction between you and your distributors, one of the three levels that I mentioned above. These are the type of questions that you should develop yourself, train extensively and use in your next sales meetings with your distributors.

Situational questions = IDENTIFY

These are chronologically the first group of questions to ask and should help you understand what is generally going on in the business of your current or potential distributor. They should help you identify which are the most important VALUES that your distributor is looking for at this time. What matters to him or her? Beware that recent changes in the business environment, developments in last year's financial results of the distributor and traumatic events in their personal life, may all lead to a significantly different appreciation of values compared to maybe just one year ago. So never take things for granted. Do not assume that you know the answer to the most relevant questions.

Here are just a few examples of situational questions:

» How is your business doing today and what is causing the deviation?
» Where would you like to be in three years from now and how do you hope to get there?
» Do you have in place today what it takes to get there? What is mainly missing?
» What are you planning to mainly invest in next year? Why is that?
» Which products will your success depend upon? What are your winners today?
» What is the one thing that you would get rid of if you could? Why is that?
» Are you happy with your current vendor relationship? What could still be improved and why does it matter to you?
» Who are your most typical customers today and why are they buying from you?

Grab the answers that you believe to matter the most to your distributor and store them in your mind. Identify the topics that you believe you will be able to respond to later in the conversation with a (hopefully unique and convincing) value proposition. You should take these relevant answers from your distributor to our next step, which is trying to quantify them.

Problem questions = QUANTIFY

Problem questions are meant to try and put a financial value on the most important values that the distributor expressed. Our ambition now is to try and quantify the answers to our situational questions that we just raised. These answers probably matter the most to us in the listening process. If managed properly and if presented in the right way, the distributor will give you an indication of the extra operational cost, the missed revenue potential, the hours of time lost, that these specific challenges mean to him.

Revealing this information to you means that a reference value, a benchmark will be put on the table for justified and fair pricing of the solution that you will present later. We will still come back to "fairness" of your pricing in a later chapter. To make the balance flip from non-purchase to purchase, you need a perceived value that is higher than the cost to acquire it. This added value to the distributor, this solution to his challenge, is what you will present at the very end under the needs statement (your value proposition).

Some examples of problem questions:

» Why was your temporary lack of inventory a problem to you? How many customers did you lose because of this? What is the average revenue of one such customer?
» Why was one week of downtime of that machine such a big problem for you? How much did it cost you? How much rent did you have to pay for that temporary replacement machine?
» Why was the waiting for 48 hours for the service intervention unacceptable? What did it cause? How would that translate into dollars?

» You mentioned that on average two service interventions per month were needed, so what is the estimated total cost then, including travel and parts?

» You are forced to hire extra storage space for six months. How much is that going to cost you?

Implementation questions = QUALIFY

After the distributor has revealed to you hopefully enough quantitative information, you understand the financial value of your upcoming proposal better. It is important in this next step to seek confirmation that the solution you are planning to suggest next, is indeed going to resolve that one specific challenge that the distributor mentioned and quantified for you. Only then, your value proposition is a strong one and should be communicated.

Some examples of implementation questions:

» If our company would be able to offer you a solution that reduces the need for inventory by 20%, how would that affect your scheduled rental of that extra storage space?

» Suppose we could offer you a service approach that would bring the intervention time down to 24 hours max, how would that help you in terms of the cost that you mentioned earlier? Would it fully resolve the issue?

» If we could deliver directly from our factory to your end-customers, would this offset the valuable service time of average five days per month that you mentioned your service team currently needs on installations and customer instructions? Would that waive the need for that extra hire for this year?

» Would your customer base grow indeed by 5% if we were able to speed up our delivery time from one week to just two days?

Needs statement = SATISFY

Now, and only now, it is time to finalize and communicate your value proposition to your distributor. Why only now? Because you have been able to pinpoint what really matters to your distributor. You have understood the value to him in case you are able to resolve these matters. And the distributor has indicated to you – without maybe even realizing this himself – the fair price that you can charge for your solution. This means that you now know what it takes to make the balance flip from the non-purchase to the purchase side. Do not lose precious time, like you probably did before, on all those other strengths of your company that add no value to the distributor.

Some examples of needs statements:

» Based on what you explained to me, I believe our "guaranteed 98% uptime" formula would absolutely work fine for you.
» Our company offers you the possibility of direct delivery to your end-customers, installation and instruction to the customer all done by our driver. And this can be done at a cost that is only half of having it done by your own service team. This would also waive the search time and cost of hiring that 50k euros extra engineer this year.

As a summary, let me compare this questions game to the well-known board game *Who is it?*. You have a pre-defined set of values that you believe you can offer to your distributors. These are represented by all the little doors in the game standing up at the very beginning of the game. During the game you will ask questions like "Is it a man?", "Does he have a beard?", "Does he have black hair?". By asking your own set of well-prepared and smart questions to your distributor, you will also be forced to close probably many of the little doors because they do not reveal any perceived value to that one distributor you are talking to. The few doors that keep standing up however are your blessing. They are the ones you will translate into a strong value proposition. And they will be the only ones that you should focus on extensively, since they do matter. If you focus more on that information sharing, including when editing your price quote, you will be more successful and sell at higher prices.

No need to say that there is a lot of homework for you to be done at this point. You cannot step into the next sales meeting with a distributor and invent relevant questions on the spot. You will have to be well prepared, work with the whole team to develop relevant questions and train them continuously on their listening skills, on relevant questions and on translating them into a convincing value proposition. This is an intense and time-consuming process that may even involve a lot of role-playing. But one that will have a huge reward, both in margin and team motivation, once it has become second nature to you and your team.

The SPIN approach in summary:

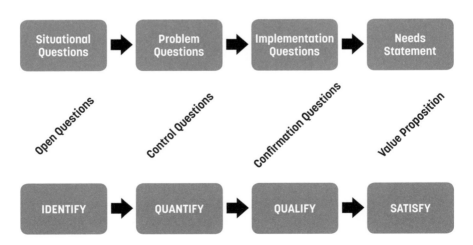

IDENTIFYING THE UNIQUE BUYING REASONS (UBRS OR USPS)

Notice that in your listening approach and by asking the right questions, you have already established a different tone in the sales process itself. No dull and inefficient comparisons of specifications anymore between you and your competitors. However, your distributors and end-customers will still play the card of competition comparison without any doubt. *"Yes, but the others have that too."*

This is because price negotiations are and will always be part of a strategic game that your distributors and end-customers want to play, as we will discuss still extensively in one of the next chapters on price negotiations. However, to minimize the risk of ending up in such unsatisfying and less profitable "price only" discussions, it is key that you work first on your Unique Selling Points (USPs), or as it is called more often these days "the Unique Buying Reasons" (UBRs). Let us first and quickly address the difference between USPs and UBRs, so we have this off the table. Both seem to refer more or less to the same but they differ in the way we think, in the starting point.

Unique Selling Points (USPs) put you as the VENDOR in the centre. You look for differentiation from competition in your products or services. The starting point here is you.

Unique Buying Reasons (UBRs) put the CUSTOMER in the centre. The starting point is what matters to them. What are the tasks the customer needs to perform and what are the gains they are looking for as well as the pains they try to avoid? How can you potentially fulfil these needs?

Based on what we discussed so far, the latter approach clearly makes more sense than USPs. Fortunately, there is a great tool available that will help you in nicely building up what should lead to your strongest value proposition. It is called "the Value Proposition Canvas".

THE VALUE PROPOSITION CANVAS

The value based selling approach and the SPIN listening technique may work well for you with potential distributors, the ones you still need to convince. But what about the distributors you already work with? How can you get a better understanding of their value perception and their needs?

The **Value Proposition Canvas** is your best starting point. It is a slightly different twist to value based selling and one that will work great with your existing distributor network. It will help you revisit all that you are currently taking for granted. It is a tool that doesn't require expensive consultancy support and one that will help you kick off an approach that your distributors will appreciate.

The same process can and should be applied on the three levels that I mentioned before:

» You towards the end-users
» You towards the distributors
» Distributors towards the end-users

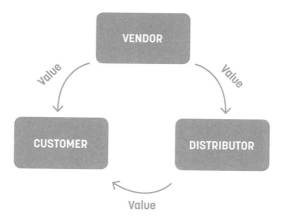

Let me give you a short background on the model and give credit to the protagonists of the Value Proposition Canvas concept.

The Value Proposition Canvas finds its origin in the Business Model Canvas by Alexander Osterwalder, published around 2010. Details and a template can be found on Wikipedia: http://bit.ly/2avQSzv.

The starting point of the Value Proposition Canvas is that companies usually put too much focus on the value that the company believes to generate itself, rather than focusing on what the customer gets out of it. In our case that customer is not only the end-user but also the distributor. And there is the relationship between distributor and end-customer.

The Value Proposition Canvas consists of two parts: the **Customer Profile** (the customer perspective) and the **Value Map** (the vendor perspective). Our objective will be to make those two fit to the maximum possible. Here is how they interact with each other:

Quality in a service or product is not what you put into it. It is what the customer gets out.
– Peter Drucker

Value map (you)

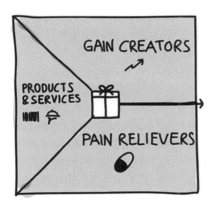

Distributor profile

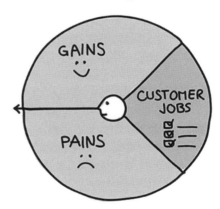

source : www.strategyzer.com

I will only zoom in here on the level between you and your distributors.

The **customer profile** describes the tasks that your distributors have to fulfil, the gains they try to get out of performing these tasks, as well as the pains they might potentially encounter in doing so. This means all that can create dissatisfaction or frustration, and therefore wants to be avoided by the distributors.

Remember how the SPIN questioning technique that we discussed will assist you strongly in understanding what generally matters most to your distributors. What adds most value to them when trying to achieve their jobs (tasks) and how can those gains and pains potentially even be quantified already through problem questions?

The **value map** starts from the position of the vendor. That is you. You define here which products and services your value proposition is built upon. You describe how they act as pain relievers against the pains of your distributors and how they will act as gain creators. So, not WHAT you offer but WHY it helps your distributors in achieving their gains and avoiding their pains when executing their tasks. And that task is primarily to represent you in the market.

Work as a team in brainstorming sessions and try to stick/remove your post-it notes into the different fields of the canvas until only the relevant ones remain.

Value map

Customer profile

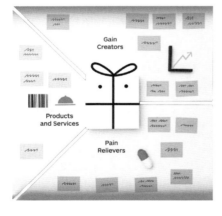

source: www.strategyzer.com

Ideally, for each post-it note that you have put on the left-hand side in your company's value map, you would be able to link it to a gain or pain on the distributor side. If not, remove it from the chart since your assumed value does not seem to fit with the distributor's need. The more lines you are able to draw, the stronger your value proposition will be for your distributors.

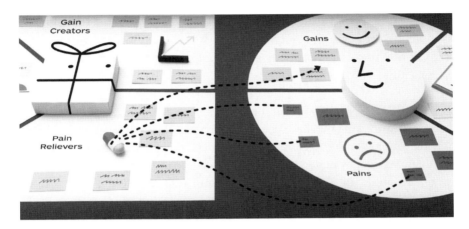

source: www.strategyzer.com

A value proposition that brings value to all or at least most of the relevant topics on the side of the customer profile is indeed a value proposition that we call a STRATEGIC FIT and will lead to increased success and higher profit margins. That is the basic idea behind the Value Proposition Canvas.

When understanding the process and after having applied it to your distributors, educate them and convince them to apply the same idea towards the end-customers. This is both from your angle as the supplier of the product and from their angle as the supplier of the local services. Your joint effort should lead to a value proposition that creates a lot of gain and strongly reduces the pain of the end-customers in the many segments that you are addressing with your distributors. What a great topic for your next international distributor meeting.

DEVELOPING THE "DISTRIBUTOR" VALUE PROPOSITION CANVAS

With distributors being our focal group in this book, I would like to zoom in exclusively here on the Value Proposition Canvas between you and your distributors. As mentioned in the beginning, some companies may – in the best case scenario – already be focusing on the value proposition of their company to the end-users. But hardly any vendor seems to sit down and explore how they can improve their value proposition to their distributors. What a pity.

It is maybe easier said than done, but definitely worth trying. It will make you feel more confident about your position towards your distributors when having your next price negotiations or when facing other challenges with them. Build trust by understanding what makes you a unique vendor to your distributor and why you deserve their full attention. And if you haven't identified anything yet that sets you apart, start working on ideas on how you could do so by starting to listen better to them in the first place and by gradually writing it down in your Value Proposition Canvas.

To assist you a little bit in the process, let me share with you how I believe distributors generally operate and think, what I believe to be their main gains and pains when trying to perform their tasks as your distributor.

DISTRIBUTOR MASLOW PYRAMID

Quite a sidestep, bringing in Maslow to make my point, but bear with me for a minute. Abraham Maslow presented his so-called "Hierarchy of Needs" in a paper in 1943. What the pyramid visualizes is that some basic needs must be fulfilled for humans to grow into the level above.

I believe the same to be true for your distributors. The reason I like to bring it up is that something interesting often takes place. When asked, we all seem to agree on the basic need of a distributor in working with us, but we hardly seem to focus or communicate with them on that basic need.

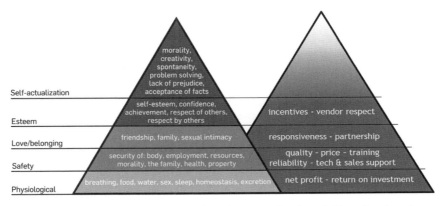

Maslow's hierarchy of needs   Distributor's hierarchy of needs

Where the analogy with Maslow applies, is that the basic need of our distributor generally is profit, it is margin. If that need is not fulfilled or maximized, then the rest may matter less to your distributors. As explained earlier under the topic of value perception, you may offer the best quality, the best service, the best training to your distributors and still not find yourself in the top position regarding focus, revenue growth and more. If they cannot generate enough return on their investment with your offering, all of your strengths may not matter to them.

Ask yourself the question how much of your communication to your distributors is related to the topic of "their" profit creation. It is very little to none. You generally talk a lot about your product features, your upcoming product launches, your next tradeshow, the next website release and the upcoming international training event. Definitely do not stop doing this, but in the end it always comes down first of all to fulfilling their basic need of making and increasing their own profit.

When your offering is not yet or no longer able to do that, distributors may start looking for alternatives to compensate for this. Alternatives do not necessarily refer to other brands of the same product types, but just other and more lucrative activities. They will however not tell you, since you may decide to find another or additional business partner for your products then. This could potentially lead to additional competition to them, so why would they even tell you? I always like to phrase it as follows: they are still taking orders but they are not selling anymore. This is the worst position you can be in as a vendor. You have become a hostage of your distributor and it is difficult to escape. They will convince you that sales are slow because the market is down, that competition is strong, that you are lacking products and of course that you are too expensive.

If distributors are not interested, it's maybe because you are not interesting.

But since you were talking too much and forgot to ask them, you may still believe to be of high interest to them. You may even believe that you can impose on them to increase focus on your products since they were granted exclusivity. But does that not feel like telling your wife that she *must* love you because you are married to each other? That's unfortunately not how relationships work. You have to earn your spot.

DISTRIBUTOR PAINS AND GAINS

The jobs (tasks) that a distributor performs can be broken down into three categories: functional, social or emotional jobs.
Examples of the different JOB categories
» Functional: delivering product to location ABC, doing product demos, training customers
» Social: developing a brand image, improving a reputation
» Emotional: creating end-customer satisfaction

PAIN describes what limits or annoys your distributor in getting the job done and what he is trying to avoid from happening.
Examples of pain:
» End-customer dissatisfaction, equipment downtime, spare parts unavailability, customers leaving the distributor, insurance claims, overtime, safety issues and more

GAIN describes what the distributor wants to achieve.

Examples of gain:

» Profit
» Easy company to work with
» Customer satisfaction
» Customer loyalty

Once again, it is important that you do your homework for your industry and put it through the test. Talk to your existing and future distributors and get confirmation what their gains and pains really are. Don't focus on your solutions but on their challenges and problems.

DISTRIBUTOR VALUE FIRST-AID KIT

Take time to sit down with your team and define the value that your company offers to your distributors. Explore their gains and pains when performing their tasks. Why do or should distributors enjoy buying from your company? The SWOT analysis that we discussed in the chapter on strategic planning should be a helpful starting point. Since you do not have time to review all of your products or solutions, focus initially on your key products and solutions, the ones that will generate most of your own margin and growth. After having selected a few, work your way down as follows:

Step 1. What are your company/product/services strengths?
(Try to exceed the level of standard answers that all competitors are listing, like "good quality", "good service" and alike.)

1   What are your product and company strengths?
    Why should distributors buy from you?

-   _____
-   _____
-   _____
-   _____
-   _____

Step 2. Which of them are your true UBRs (USPs)? Or still, what sets you apart from most other vendors?

2. Which of your strengths are unique and set you apart from others?
   - _____
   - _____
   - _____
   - _____
   - _____

Step 3. How do these UBRs (USPs) translate into value for the distributor? Or still: what's in it for them? Be very critical and after every answer raise the question "SO WHAT?" until you have converted the unique offering into a true and measurable value for the distributor.

3. How do these UBRs (USPs) translate into value for your distributor? What's in it for them?
   - _____
   - _____
   - _____
   - _____
   - _____

Further down this section I will help you with a first-aid kit of values that I believe your distributors are generally looking for. For your end-customers you need to work with the market intelligence that you have developed typically for your industry.

Step 4. Now translate your value into a formal value proposition to your distributor.

Here I will again try to take you to another level than the standard value propositions you may hear or read. Today, the companies that stand out are the ones that have understood the power of storytelling.

THE POWER OF STORYTELLING

In their book *Made to Stick* Chip and Dan Heath explain how you can build a story that will survive others that die and how you can make it stick. I will limit myself to the highest possible level of summary of the book, which is the acronym "SUCCESs". When you have developed a value proposition for your distributors but also when communicating to the market in general, a list of just six criteria can make the difference between having a story that everybody will forget or one that will stick. The acronym is SUCCES(s) and stands for:

Simple

Unexpected

Concrete

Credible

Emotional

Story

Allow me to use a simple example from my current industry and company, which is Hyundai Construction Equipment, one of the strong market players in excavators, wheel loaders and forklifts. When offering a unique 360° viewing monitor that makes all blind spots around our huge and most powerful wheel loaders visible, I could explain to the distributors and end-users what it does and how we technically achieve this unique feature. Or I can have one of the end-customers present their true story about how one of their workers got killed six months ago when being ran over by one of the wheel loaders (from a brand that did not have this visualization system). There was an article in the local newspaper about that customer, their good reputation on safety that was hurt, the legal issue that will take months still to be resolved. What will impact on the reader the most, you think?

When using proof, when having distributors talk about the experience with your company and how it impacted on their business or maybe even their personal life, you will have a value proposition to potential distributors that will stick. In line with my earlier statement "stop selling, start listening", I could potentially add:

> Stop selling, start telling.

IT STARTS WITH WHY

To close the value based selling approach I am going to bring in one of my other inspiring authors and heroes that I mentioned in my preface. His name is Simon Sinek. I can highly recommend his Tedx 2009 presentation, titled "It starts with why". His presentation made me aware that we all make that same mistake. We tend to talk to our dealers and customers a lot about WHAT we do, what we offer and HOW we do it. But, in general we never get to the WHY we do it. Reverse the order (start with why) and you will be more convincing to your distributors and end-users. You will sell VALUE this way and you will sell at much higher profit margins.

I have deliberately kept the "it starts with why" for last because I wanted you to first understand the basics of value selling and the importance of storytelling. If you have reached the expert level on both these topics, I believe you are ready to close the loop and go back to the drawing table for your strategic plan 2.0. Rethink your vision, mission and everything else in your strategic and marketing plan, based on the new insights you have developed in your value selling and storytelling exercises. Trust me. It will set you apart from many of your competitors. Mingle with the grazing cows and find little grass that is left or choose your separate spot in the field and find a lot of grass, just for you.

In tender markets, it is all about price and nothing of the above will apply, right? Wrong. I have heard that excuse so many times from distributors and salespeople who prefer to choose the road of the least resistance, which is asking just for lower prices.

Once again, the primary need of a distributor is to make profit. So you cannot blame them for trying to get some of that profit from you, the vendor. This is much easier for the distributor than trying to sell himself at higher prices to an end-customer. It is also less risky for them than potentially losing the deal against a more competitive offering from another brand to that same target end-customer, agreed?

Respect the attempt, but don't walk into the trap. Tender business is not only about price, although professional purchasing departments will make it look like that to you and your distributors. When analysing tenders, particularly after you and your distributors have won them, you will learn that price is important indeed. But in general there are at least three or more other parameters that influence the customer's decision. So here is what you should remember.

> 90% of all tenders you win before
> they are even issued.

That is a strong statement, but one that makes sense. Companies successfully winning tenders are the ones that manage to influence the potential buyer before the text of the tender is even written. Winners work pro-actively and closely with the buying department and users, they understand what adds value to them, they know how their company can offer value and they help the purchasing department in writing the specifications for the tender. Or at least, they indicate what should definitely be included in the scoring system. Do you remember that last tender that felt like it was written for that one competitor? They did the job. If your distributors have not been involved in the process at all, if they have not been able to understand what the customer is trying to resolve or wants to achieve, then price may be the only thing left to fight with indeed. And purchasing departments will be happy to use your low price offer against the one they actually want to work with from the beginning. So not offering at all, is sometimes an even better option. It may save you time and frustration.

Remember what I told you at the beginning of this book about market segmentation, about the profile of your distributors and their market coverage, about them having access to your target segments, decision makers and everything else on that matter. If the match is not correct, if your tender customers are not frequently visited by your distributors and with the right sales approach, then YOU will be the one being forced to sell to your distributor at a lower price for HIM to still make that wanted profit. Doesn't sound right, does it? However, this is exactly what happens too many times to too many companies that are selling in tender markets.

Improve the world but start with yourself. Before being able to convince distributors that even in tender markets you can sell based on value, start by showing yourself how to do this properly. Next, develop and provide to them all the tools possible to convince tender customers on why you do what you do and how your distributor will provide them with the right solutions, how it helps resolving their challenges. That is your job. The job of the distributor is to work on the contact, to get meeting time well in advance to the issuing of the tender, to be aware of when that next tender will be issued and everything else that you may expect from a strong distributor.

TRAINING, TRAINING, TRAINING

What one does is what counts and not what one had the intention of doing.
– Pablo Picasso

It is generally known that without intense training, including role-playing, most of the knowledge acquired will be lost. All will remain a mere intention and nothing will happen. Do not walk into that trap either. Extensively train your own team and do the same with your distributors. Use your dealer events to do so. You will both benefit from it, no longer just the end-customer with lower pricing.

Managing objections

Earlier in the book I explained why customers do or don't buy from you and how you can and should influence their perception. You have also learned the basics of value based selling. In a perfect world all the distributors that you speak to after today, would all buy from you at premium prices and with no tough questions asked. That of course is utopia and it is not going to happen.

Sales are not a positive science or algorithm that you can activate each time again and with guaranteed success. You are dealing with people, with businessmen and -women, with emotions. Your distributors will bring objections to the table whenever they can and whenever it suits them. Your task is to handle them in the most efficient way. And some basic tips and tricks can do the job for you.

Here is some good news to start with. Distributors that share objections with you are more valuable to you than those who don't speak and just walk away. Not physically walking away that is, but by not focusing enough on your products anymore. This is what I referred to earlier as still taking orders but no longer selling. It is the worst situation that you can be in and the most difficult one to get out of.

Great account managers love distributor objections since satisfying them brings them a step closer to the next order.

Distributor objections are generally related to the following topics:

> **Price**
> **Quality**
> **Service**
> **Competition**
> **Experience**
> **... and other**

Price is absolutely the main objection. And let me surprise you, it should be! As I will mention later, if price is never brought up by your distributors as an objection, then you are definitely TOO CHEAP. Increase your prices immediately after finishing this book and you will make some easy money. It is the easiest way to increase your margin with virtually zero risk.

OBJECTION OR COMPLAINT

One thing that you need to understand before we discuss how to handle distributor objections is the difference between an objection and a complaint. Try to answer quickly yourself before you continue. Here's the difference and why it matters.

> » **Objection** = a perception that prevents your distributor from buying
> » **Complaint** = a true problem, something that happened and is not supposed to happen

The reason that the difference matters is because they require a different approach. They must be tackled differently.

> **Objection** = a perception that prevents a distributor from buying more
>
> → use the listening and questioning skills that we developed, bring arguments and proof to the table to change the perception
>
> **Complaint** = a true problem, something that happened and is not supposed to happen
>
> → resolve it, fix the reported problem and get confirmation from your distributor that it is considered fixed

HOW TO HANDLE DISTRIBUTOR OBJECTIONS

A good 7-step approach to handling objections is the following. It also fits nicely in our value based selling understanding that we developed earlier. It will perfectly do the job if applied properly.

1	Listen (what does the distributor mean exactly?)
2	Reduce tension (show understanding)
3	Ask questions (what is the base for it?)
4	Separate real from false (will resolution change their decision?)
5	Separate real from misunderstanding
6	Present (new) proof (references, documents…)
7	Agree (get confirmation that objection has been resolved now)

As I have and will mention again several times in this book, distributors should be looked at through two different lenses. They are a customer AND they are an extension of your own organization. In both cases they deserve to be heard and treated properly. Their feedback is valuable information to the whole vendor organization. It generates input that can help you grow into being an even better and more profitable supplier to them. Unfortunately, only few companies do share distributor objections internally between the proper stakeholders and in a well-structured way. And only few will work on process or product improvement based on that valuable distributor input. In the best-case scenario, they will just resolve issues on a need base and move on with the daily business. What a missed opportunity!

On point 1 (listen to what your distributor means) I do remember the funny but not unrealistic example of one of my trainees who was called by a distributor who told him: "Frank, I want to inform you that our competitor ABC have just dropped their prices by 5%." Frank, the account manager, responded within seconds: "George, let me see what I can do for you on our price." The distributor kept quiet for a few seconds, laughed and then responded that he was not after a better price but just wanted to inform him, "as valuable market input only". The trainee felt incredibly stupid about his unprofessional response to the distributor. He took the road of the least resistance there and almost lost margin for no reason. And he should feel stupid. Sometimes we just fail to listen to what is being said, since we are assuming things and are already thinking too much about our answer. Again, we change to talking mode too quickly.

An objection is not a rejection.
It is simply a request for more information.

– Bo Bennett

PRICE is the most common objection, and it should be. It is probably my favourite topic in managing distributors and the one that can generate the most profit for you as a vendor, if handled properly. In the next chapters, we will therefore spend valuable time on how to get more (margin) out of your distributors.

PRICE, AN OBJECTION OR A COMPLAINT?

Based on the differences that I explained to you, are comments from your distributors on your pricing an objection now or rather a complaint? (Give yourself a few seconds to think about the answer to that one.)

Right, it can be both. A glass of water at five euros in the middle of the desert may be perceived as expensive or even a rip-off, but it definitely holds that value when no alternative is available to you after three days of walking with no sign of life. If offered at that same five euros price in a regular bar, next to another one with no difference in seating, interior, same brand of water, it may be a complaint since that bar owner has absolutely nothing available to justify the huge difference in price for exactly the same value to the visiting customer.

As discussed in the chapter on value based selling, the secret in maximizing your distributor and end-user pricing is by trying to exactly move the price discussion away from such one on one comparison with the offering of your competition. On the other hand, if too high pricing is a justified customer complaint, then fixing that problem is unfortunately the only right solution. Or you can decide not to adjust and accept just whichever order that you may get at that price (high margin with low volume). We will do some mathematics around that volume-price decision in the next chapter.

A realistic and typical example of such price complaint could be the sales of genuine spare parts (guaranteed original) through your web shop at double the price of an alternative channel offering exactly the same. It could end up being a true complaint if that alternative channel offers exactly the same delivery speed, delivery quality, product warranty and can proof that their products are also the original ones, just like yours. Some companies just apply a standard mark-up for all of their parts and without differentiating between what is commonly available on the market versus own developments. Many times distributors will decide to buy elsewhere in that case. And you cannot blame them for it.

Reverse your way of thinking and you can actually make it work to your advantage. As a golden rule I like to suggest that whatever a distributor can easily compare, offer it with lower margins and target high volume. It will not only generate volume but also strongly support the image, the distributor perception, that all of your spare parts pricing is probably fair, including the ones they cannot really compare. Make your higher margin on those items that are more difficult to compare or physically more difficult to get in the marketplace. We will come back to this later.

Distributor pricing and margin

Before addressing negotiation techniques to use when negotiating prices with distributors, let us first address the importance of your price positioning. List prices, discounts, customer net prices, all of them have an important meaning and should be handled with equal care. The statement that in the end, the only thing that matters is what the end-users pay net, is incorrect. All of the elements in the pricing and discounting process have a different and important meaning.

Let us list a few and explain the relevance of each of them.

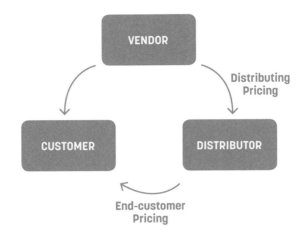

DISTRIBUTOR LIST PRICE

I am referring here to your probably annual or more frequently updated standard pricelist to your distributors. This pricelist may differ by region (e.g. due to different negotiation culture or due to very significant differences in the net market pricing which would potentially lead to unrealistically high percent discounts in specific countries.

Some may claim the list price to be irrelevant but I fully disagree. The list price to your dealer indicates how each of your products and services are positioned against competition and against other products in your portfolio (e.g. a former model of the same product).

It also creates an important reference point to larger distributors on what the expected standard price is that their smaller peer distributors will probably pay in full for the same product.

In general, this pricing is determined by the marketing management of the vendor.

DISTRIBUTOR NET PRICE

This is what the distributor will pay net to the vendor, based on standard or ad hoc discounts that are granted to them. It acts as a reference point for the gross margin the distributor will be able to make locally and for the margin you will make as the vendor.

It is generally decided by sales management. Your challenge is to find the right balance between your earnings and those of the distributor. Unfortunately, companies often have not enough insight in the latter. You may be lowering your pants while the distributor is still making good money.

END-USER LIST PRICE

Like your list price to the distributor, this is the way for the distributor to position his offering against the local competition. It represents the value that he believes to create for the average end-customer.

It also acts to the market as a reference point to what a smaller end-customer will potentially pay for the product or service with no discount granted.

It should always be highest possible to create a high value perception to the end-users and to create a good span for price negotiation where needed. The task of the distributor is to create and influence the perceived value to the end-customer.

In general, this is a distributor management responsibility, sometimes in alignment with vendor recommended pricing.

END-USER NET PRICE

This is the expression of the value perception by the end-customer. It is the amount the end-customer is willing to pay for the distributor's offering and for the value perceived by that individual customer.

It determines the gross margin the distributor will make on the individual deals with all of his customers.

DISTRIBUTOR MARGIN

Price is what you pay. Value is what you get.

– Warren Buffett

It is the difference between the net price charged by the vendor and the net price the end-customer is willing to pay to the distributor. It is the gross amount the distributor has available to pay for all of his costs, needed to sell, deliver and support your product.

NET PROFIT MARGIN

What the distributor will earn in the end is the main reason why distributors are willing to represent your products and solutions. This is what creates the highly needed "share of mind" and continued interest to represent your company and work hard for you.

If the net margin of distributors is no longer interesting, they will no longer be interested. But they will not tell you. I repeat: they will still be taking orders but they are not selling anymore. The worst situation you can be in as a vendor.

I want to stress here, in defence of the distributors, that sometimes vendors do underestimate the investments needed to sell your product. You invest in research and development, in logistics, marketing tools and more. But your distributors, if performing like you like them to, also have a lot of costs and risks. They need to invest in the customer relationship, local marketing communication, customer events, tradeshows, product presentation, product installation, end-user training, aftersales service, regulations, product recovery at end of lifetime and much more. Try to assess the total investment needed by your distributors if you want to take the right decision on what is a fair net profit margin for them on your portfolio.

Negotiating prices with distributors

Price discussions are standard in doing business with distributors. I hope that by now you have come to understand why that is. They are after profit margin in the first place. They are not there to "serve" you. They will try to get the margin from their end-customers but also from you, the vendor. They are professional business people like yourself, so you cannot blame them for trying to do so.

I see companies spending hours trying to calculate their exact cost prices, their expected profit margin by item, deciding on a fair dealer list price while at the same time, at the end of the chain, sales is so easily giving that one percent extra discount still to that large distributor. That's a pity. Sometimes it is because distributors have become so powerful and important to you, that they have basically taken over the business from you. Or, you have a sales team that likes to walk the road of the least resistance. This means they spend more time convincing their own management to lower prices than to work on the distributors themselves. Sometimes friendships that have developed between sales people and the distributor are at the base of this attitude. It may also be driven by fear that bonus targets will not be achieved. It can be based on disbelieve in the quality of the products that one represents. Many reasons exist indeed why sales people give up too easily on their good pricing and lack the pride to maximize pricing. What I try to prove to trainees every time is the huge impact this may have on the bottom line of the company, particularly if your margins are already on the lower side.

One approach is the following. When a sales person approaches you, the sales manager, and claims that lower pricing is needed, make them calculate for you how much volume (units) needs to be sold more at this lower price to maintain your total margin in value.

Let us do a quick calculation example:

» Target quantity this year for distributor A: 1000 units
» Unit cost price to you (vendor): 800€
» Net sales price to distributor A: 1000€
» Distributor A requests a 5% lower price from you

Question: How many units should distributor A sell more so you maintain your total € target gross margin in case we do accept this 5% lower price request?

Answer: 33.3% more volume! (Yes, indeed!)

Calculation
» Target profit margin per unit: 1000€ - 800€ = 200€
» Target number of units: 1000 units
» Target gross margin: 1000 units x 200€ margin = 200,000€ margin

Profit margin with new pricing: 950€ - 800€ = 150€

Units needed: 200,000€ target margin / 150€ = 1333 units = +33.3%

An amazing 33.3% volume increase (and equally more effort) is needed to achieve your target gross margin for just a 5% price decrease in this example. Let us also add to this shock by indicating that the impact is even bigger since price decreases are not that easy to recover from. So the impact will exist over the following years as well.

Companies live from leftover, not from turnover

Here is another approach. When annually raising your prices to distributors and getting objections from your team, make them calculate how much volume you may lose due to this price increase and still make the same margin in value. Reality almost every time is that the risk of losing customers over any little price increase is virtually zero. This is unless you have completely failed to sell your value to your distributors or end-customers. Distributors that are representing your brand since many years will not just walk away because of your next little price increase.

Example
» Target quantity this year for distributor A: 1000 units
» Unit cost price to you (vendor): 800 €
» Current net sales price to distributor A: 1000€
» Planned price increase next year: +2%

Question: How many units can we lose (sell less) to the distributor due to the price increase and still make the same total gross margin?

Answer: 9.1% less volume

Calculation
» Current profit margin per unit: 1000€ - 800€ = 200€
» New profit margin per unit: 1020€ - 800€ = 220€
» Volume needed for same total margin: 200,000€ / 220€ = 909 units

Or still, if the small price increase leads to less than 9.1% drop in volume in this example, we are improving our gross margin. Assess with your team the risk of losing this high 9.1% volume because of just a 2% price increase. I think you know the answer already now.

Revenue is Vanity.
Profit is Sanity.
Cash Flow is Reality.

Stop being afraid. Distributors cannot just go and tell the market that for ten or more years they have been representing the wrong brand. Just like it is difficult for you to change or acquire new distributors, it is also difficult for them to completely change to another vendor. So don't be scared to adapt your pricing at least annually while monitoring of course all that we have discussed so far. Are they adding the necessary value to maximize their own end-user pricing? How is their end-user pricing changing? What is your own market intelligence on competition market pricing? Are you a market leader or rather a small follower? And everything else there is to know to make a smart decision and be in the driver seat on distributor pricing.

BE PROUD TO BE EXPENSIVE

Experience shows that being slightly more expensive is actually a more comfortable position to be in. You are addressing the more interesting market segment to start with, but it also creates more certainty on the side of the customer. It supports the perception that you like to create and it is easier to defend as a sales person compared to a low price offering. Lower pricing is always more suspicious. What is the catch? Why is your brand so cheap? What am I overlooking as a customer that I may regret after my purchase? Low pricing is many times a confirmation that a company does not add value or that at least it is not able to convey its value proposition to the distributor or end-customer.

Distributors that you win on price, you often lose for the same reason.

Ask your existing distributors on a regular base how they feel about you as a company. It can help you in becoming slightly more arrogant as a vendor (and distributor) and to not position yourself too low on price. You will attract the wrong distributors with too low price positioning.

WHY DISTRIBUTORS DISCUSS PRICE

There are several reasons why this happens. Next to what I explained already as their way to gain margin also from you, there may be other reasons. Using your SPIN listening skills and asking the right questions can help you find the answers and appropriate response.

Some will discuss price with you because they simply do not want to push your product anymore but are afraid or unwilling to tell you. Keep this in mind also when talking to a new potential distributor. They may long have decided to stay with their current vendor but will be happy to get low pricing from you to push their existing vendor down. Do not lose precious time on these kind of games and delay your price quotes as long as possible in the negotiation.

It may be a way for distributors to get compensation for dissatisfaction that they have. Product problems may have created high costs on their end and they seek payback. If you fail to understand this and adapt your pricing for this wrong reason, you will continue to pay for many years to come if you have to build up your pricing again over time from a lower level. Compensation for justified complaints should be handled in a different way, not through discounts or price decreases.

Distributors may also have a general cost structure problem and need to improve their financial situation. By asking the right questions and listening to what is being said, other solutions than price discounts may come to the table. It may include changes in payment terms or even business model.

Some large distributors will discuss price because they have a purchasing department with people that are paid to do so. It is their daily task to review pricing with vendors, even if you have already the best price on the planet. They are often incentivized for any price reduction they can achieve.

And in some regions like e.g. the Middle East, negotiation is strongly integrated in the business culture. Not giving a discount may even be perceived as an insult. Some industry segments may also have a discounting culture. Take it into account when setting your list prices and play the game wherever needed.

TIPS AND TRICKS FOR PRICE NEGOTIATIONS

There are hundreds of books and articles out there on price negotiations in general, so I will limit myself to some statements that apply strongly to price discussions with distributors. See them as your checklist to review before stepping into your next negotiation.

» Always come prepared to distributor price negotiations. Run scenarios upfront and calculate the impact in advance.
» Understand correctly any price change request from a distributor before responding to it.

» Collect your own market price information to strengthen your own negotiation position.

» Avoid structural price changes that have an impact over several years.

» Take time to respond to price change requests, even if it's easy for you to just say yes. It confirms the seriousness and the impact of such a request on your company results. It confirms that this is something that shouldn't be asked too often.

» Avoid quick email or call replies and preferably have a higher level person in the organization respond to the request. This way you show that internal discussion was needed to come to an agreement on this.

» First confirm verbally that the new price will conclude the deal, resolves the issue or whatever the reason for the request was. Only then confirm in writing to avoid that your price quote will be used for the wrong reason (e.g. just pushing pricing of the current vendor to the distributor further down).

» Dare to say NO to selected deals. It will show your distributor that a threshold has been reached.

» Think total margin. Understand the sometimes huge impact on volume and margin when agreeing to even small discounts. This rule particularly applies in business with small percentage margins.

» Add something instead of discounting. This way you will maintain the base price of your product. You confirm that there is no room left in the margin and you can push other strategic products by including them. Add for example a consumable to the capital equipment that you also want the distributor to sell more of.

» Always get something in return. There is no such thing as a free lunch. Have your distributor commit to a contractual purchase volume or other formal commitments that compensate for your effort.

» Share the burden. When market pricing forces prices down it cannot just be you, the vendor, that absorbs the pain.

» Open calculation. In case of large projects get written confirmation and proof of the prices that the distributor applies to his end-customer. Secure this way a fair balance in pain between you and the distributor.

» Dare to challenge the distributor on the value of your distributor agreement. In the end you have decided to work with them since you expected to achieve a certain price-volume combination. Their request for lower pricing is in a way a unilateral cancellation of that agreement and can be presented as such to them in the discussion.

» Stay professional at all times. Never insult or show disrespect to a distributor when he comes to you for the next price discount. It is a strategic game that you can win if you play if right.

NEVER GIVE A DISCOUNT

Dutch author and speaker Jos Burgers is a guru who has inspired me a lot on performing better price negotiations. I had the pleasure of joining one of his inspiring training sessions. His book *Geef nooit korting!* (Never Give a Discount!) unfortunately is not available in English. So I will quote some of his statements and hope they will help you in your next price discussions, both internally with your sales team as with distributors.

Make sure that you are not too busy if your margins are small

Many business people complain that they are extremely busy, have to work very hard and have to live from very small margins. What a stupid position to be in. Go back to my examples above and see how you can be less busy by increasing your prices rather than discounting. If your margin is low today and you increase your price significantly, you may have a lot less work and still make the same margin in value. Think about it.

Discounting too fast sends the wrong message

If you discount too easily and too fast since you want to secure the deal, you are basically telling your distributor that you were trying to take some money from him, but it looks like the plan is not going to work this time. Giving discounts too fast confirms that there was indeed enough air for you to manoeuvre, that there is good profit for you in the deal. But it also triggers the question on the side of the distributor whether he got enough discount for himself out of the deal. So he will probably try to get even more because of your quick response.

Reverse your thinking from price discounting to price increases

As I indicated in my examples above, your mind should be set standard on how you can achieve and justify price increases on a regular base. This requires good understanding of the value based selling techniques that I explained to you. But from now on, any year without a price increase for whichever product should be considered a missed opportunity. Do the mathematics for yourself and see what 1 to 2% increase does to your bottom line and do a risk assessment of how much business you can afford to lose and still make the same profit as the year before while working less hard yourself.

If you are never too expensive, you are without any doubt too cheap

As I indicated already, pricing should be a discussion topic. Also when evaluating distributor satisfaction, they should not give you a good score on pricing. If they say that they buy from you because of your good prices or the good price-quality ratio, then your prices are probably too low. Have the courage to increase immediately and be pleasantly surprised by the little impact it will have on your sales volume.

But we are already so expensive

Pick one person in your organization. Let us use Frank again. Agree that each of you will go to Frank any time today. The first person will tell him he looks a little pale today, the second asks him whether he is okay. The third asks a similar question on how he feels. After three or four people asking him, no doubt Frank will walk over to the restroom, look at himself in the mirror and agree that maybe today he does not look very sharp. The message behind this story is that if your team keeps repeating enough times that you are too expensive, at the end you *will* be, because everyone will start believing it. So, avoid the self-fulfilling prophecy, this complaining and disbelief in your own strengths. Fight it at all times and change the perception. Did not hundreds of customers decide to buy from you anyway? Were they all wrong?

Do not duck before you get hit

Too many sales people give discounts too quickly. Too often do they assume already upfront that they will be too expensive. This is because the distributor claims that he will lose the project. We assume way too often that what distributors say on price is correct and like boxers we duck before we get hit. Remember that distributors have no interest in telling you the full truth on market pricing and on their own net pricing to end-users.

Learn from your existing customers

Our price decisions are often driven by the projects that we lost, seldom by the ones that we did win alright. Only few companies take enough time to talk to existing end-customers. Try to find out from them why they did buy from you, how you were able to be of value to them and whether they are satisfied about your and your distributor's performance. This should help you understand what fair pricing for your products and solutions really is.

The many meanings of too expensive

When being told that you are too expensive, many other statements can be hidden behind that single phrase. Responding with a discount may not even solve the problem. Remember that painter that made you a price offer last time you couldn't refuse. But you didn't like his face and you thought he was not properly dressed. Telling him that he was too expensive saved you from having to work with him, although he was the cheapest. And did you not say on that other occasion that the price was too high while you really meant that you didn't have the budget available at that time for that investment? Also here asking the right questions will help you identify other replies to the "too expensive" statement that can get you the deal without giving a discount.

Check the outcome before giving a discount

Before giving a discount to e.g. a new distributor, get confirmation that it will change his buying decision. Only then confirm the discount. In case of the painter above that got the "No, thank you, too expensive" it would not be wise to just offer a lower price. Instead he should ask whether a lower price would change your decision to work with him. You would probably still say "no" and the painter has a chance to find out through smart questions which reason other than price is influencing your negative perception.

If you do discount, always give a reason

In the cases where you believe a discount is fair and needed, always give a firm reason why you do it. It can be stock you want to move, the precious relationship with your dealer that you value or whatever other reason. But give a valuable one. Never just "give" a discount.

HOW TO PRESENT YOUR PRICES

Following our basic education on value selling, allow me to advise you also on how to best put your price quotes together. Then educate your distributors on doing the same.

First, through the SPIN questions you should have been able to figure out what adds most value to your distributor or end-customer. Make sure that you stress those items in your pricelists or price quotes. Elaborate more on the value topics in the quote and stress how it responds to his or her needs. Also remember to address the why question and the quantification of your value wherever possible.

Undress your price. Improve the perception of value in your price communication by breaking down your price into all of the value adding items. Even if you ship the product for free, if you install it for free, if you train the end-customer for free, always make sure that you list all of these items. Put a price value on it and then indicate that it is included, discounted for 100% or whatever makes sense. This way your distributor or their end-customer will understand that the price for the base unit itself is actually very fair. The other effect is that you may create uncertainty around the "all-in" price quote from competition. Are all of your value items included in their offering as well? Why are they not mentioning it?

If you offer multiple solutions to the distributor's need, present them from most expensive to cheaper. It is proven that when presented this way, customers will mentally bear with you longer if you start with your flagship and offer cheaper alternatives than when you are starting with a base model and making it more and more expensive with more and more features being brought to the table as you move on in the presentation.

I realize that on many of the topics above you may respond with an "I knew all of that". Still, we tend to forget it when stepping into our price discussions. So hopefully next time when you prepare for an important one, you will open these pages again and save yourself a few unnecessary discounts and unneeded loss of margin.

Let me close this chapter with a statement that says it all:

> Distributors in general do not leave you for price. They leave you for lack of attention.

The fight for share of mind

WHO ARE YOUR COMPETITORS?

If I ask you to list your main competitors, I am fairly sure that you will give me the names of the established brands that you and your distributors are fighting against in your industry. They are the ones that make you fail from time to time in a deal. You will probably also state that when this happened, it was in general because of price. This is at least what the distributor has been telling you.

In the chapter on value based selling I hope that you have learned that selling against competition can be replaced by selling your own value to individual customers or distributors. You have also learned how you can improve the way you negotiate prices with distributors and end-customers. But, the next thing to understand is that the leading brands in your industry are NOT your most important competitors. It is the other products or solutions that your distributors are selling.

No need to say that the overall performance of your distributors – as your representatives – will largely influence your chances of success. It will be influenced by their listening skills, by their understanding of value based selling, their service performance, networking capabilities and so many other things. But do not forget what we said on the basic needs of your distributors. The primary interest of most of your distributors is to generate profit. They will look for ways to generate this profit in the easiest way possible. They will focus their sales teams on the products and solutions that will bring the big money to their bank. And you cannot blame them for that. This is normal business practice.

So from now on, you need to understand that your competition is not those other established brands. It is everything else that your distributor is selling. You are in a continuous fight for "share of wallet" and "share of mind".

SHARE OF WALLET

When we discussed the distributor profile, I indicated that you should not be looking for the biggest size distributor. You should rather try to identify the ones that need your product badly to strategically complete their portfolio. You need the ones that show willingness to fight for your products. If ever you would discontinue your partnership, there should be pain felt on their side. Their wallet should feel the difference if this would ever happen. That's when you have the right size and profile of distributor, we did agree.

Your challenge is to be the notes in the wallet of the distributor, not the change. My own change after shopping always ends up in my piggy bank, not in the wallet that I carry close to my heart. The change remains untouched until I really need it or when I check whether it is still there.

It is a fight for share of wallet. You should understand what your share is in the revenue of your distributor. Or even better, what is your share in their profit. If it is their change, their little extra, then how can you ever expect a distributor to work hard for you? They are after the bigger money and being professional business people they should be.

SHARE OF MIND

It is not only about the money in the wallet. It all starts with getting on the radar of your distributor. It is about getting their attention. I like to call it the generation of sparks in the heads of the distributors. And this is at the different levels in their organization, from management to sales and marketing and logistics. It should include all people that play a role in getting your product successfully to the end-customers.

Let us bring the Value Proposition Canvas back to the table here again. Understand what are the gains that each of them are after and the pains that they encounter in selling your product. Understand how you can add value as a vendor to each of them and address those issues in your sales contacts. This is how you create share of mind. This is what will make distributors work harder for you. This is why regular visits to your distributors are so important. See what is really going on at their site, which banners are displayed in their showroom, which products are mainly stored in the warehouse. Try to understand what their mind is really focused on. This is your true competition, not the established brands that you believe to lose against usually on price.

CREATING SHARE OF MIND

I called the book "The Channel Whisperer" not because I feel like a guru but because I believe that on many of the topics that we have discussed, the distributor is not the one to blame or to change. It is in the first place about you and your company. Making your distributors work harder for you is in your own hands. It is in the way you manage your distributorships.

Distributors in general will not leave you because of price. They will rather leave you for a lack of attention. Sit back for a second and critically review what you have done for each of your individual distributors in the past year to generate those highly needed sparks in their heads. Not enough, probably.

You may think that the international distributor meeting that you did in January will have had a big impact. Maybe so, but two weeks later the vendor of the other products they are selling did exactly the same. And so will the third one next month. You will be forgotten and off the radar sooner than you think.

You send them regular newsletters but do you read everything you receive in your mailbox? Do you read it immediately and do you always forward it to the ones that should know? Nope. It is no different with your distributors. They do not serve you. They chose their own priorities and will not always come and tell you what they are. When you visit them, when you ask them, you will probably walk away with the feeling that you are their "numero uno". And you probably even are at the day of your visit. If you are not on the other days, then you will hear in the first place that the market is extremely difficult, that you have a lot of things going wrong in your company and – guess what? – that again you are also way too expensive.

Here is a first-aid kit with the most relevant actions that you can take to gain share of mind. The list is not exhaustive, not ranked in order of importance, but hopefully it inspires you at least to just focus on share of mind more often with your team from now on.

Profit

Maybe start in the first place by changing your mindset from your product quality and service to distributor value and profit. Continuously ask yourself the questions: What is in it for my distributor? How does it add to their revenue and profit generation? How can we improve our processes, product installation cost, training cost, parts cost and more to improve the potential profit that our distributors and you can make? This is probably the most important one in your generation of sparks, in getting your spot on their radar on a continuous base. And show them explicitly that you care.

Organization

We discussed mainly the profile of your sales team earlier in the book. But no need to say that everyone in your company that interacts with your distributor plays a key role in keeping your distributor satisfied. Do a quick run and evaluate for each of your distributors who is looking after them and how they perform. Try to excel. Have your distributors also evaluate your team's performance. After all, the distributors are not only an extension of your organization but also your customers. Not companies do business but people do. If you have a team that is competent and engaged, then again you will get more sparks on the radar of your distributors.

Investment

Make it easier for your distributors to get your product to the market. And I mean that in the broad sense of the word. They want to generate their profit in the easiest way possible. If you can reduce the investments needed on their side, if you can help them increase the hit rate, if the service needs on your product can be lowered, if you can do more training through Skype to reduce their travel expenses and time off, then they will like you more. Have the courage to sit down and do the cost calculation for their side of the equation also from time to time. Try to understand the investments needed by the distributor to get your product presented, sold, delivered, trained and serviced to the end-customer. Does your offering give the best possible return on investment and how does it possibly compare to that other product range they are selling from that other company? What is the effort needed there and the profit generated?

Predictability

Distributors do not like surprises. I have been in many meetings with logistics departments where delivery times are being discussed. One thing I have learned by listening more to distributors is that they fully understand that sometimes things go wrong internally. But what distributors really need is predictability. They like to work with vendors that can commit to a delivery time and stick to it, even when they wished it in general to be shorter. They dislike vendors that give them updates on a daily basis and see the expected date of delivery change back and forth every time. They prefer to work with a vendor that maybe standard needs that one week more than the competition, but at least is predictable and trustworthy.

Distributors know perfectly well how to handle unfavourable delivery time information with their end-customer at the time of their purchase. But repeated and unreliable updates on that promised date and having to go back to that same end-customer over and over again with more unfavourable news is what kills the sparks on the radar. And of course this does not apply just to delivery dates but also to predictability on price changes, notification periods, contract reviews, training events and alike.

Ease of mind

Try to be or become that best company to do business with. Embrace your distributors as a customer. And I am not referring here to easily giving them discounts when they ask and not to giving them whatever they ask for. What distributors like to see is that complaints, product returns and requests for information are always picked up and handled in a quick and professional way. They can trust that it will be answered in a timely way and sent to the right persons. Nobody on their side needs to check ten times and send reminders. It is taken care of. It should be like ordering a dress online, getting that new dress sent in time, not really liking it after all, simply dropping the sealed box off again in one of the selected stores, getting your money refunded within three working days and all of this without having to worry for one second about the whole process. That is probably today's expectation also on the side of the distributors in doing business with you.

Time to the first sale

Particularly with new distributors but also with new products it is key that the product does sell easily. If after the kick-off of a new distributorship or the launch of new products through your channels they do experience repeated difficulties in selling it, then you can keep pushing as hard as you'd like but in reality they will focus less on that product or try to sell it more on price to still make the necessary margin. They will be taking orders but will not be selling. Train them, assist them, but strive to make it as easy as possible for them to achieve those first sales. This again will put you on their radar. It will create the necessary share of mind.

Hit rate

Linked to the previous one is the hit rate for your products in general. How many customers need to be visited? How many quotes need to be sent to close one successful deal? How can you generate more sales leads yourself on your corporate site? Generating valuable leads and converting the highest possible number of them into profitable sales, is what your conversion strategy should be about.

Repeat sales

Distributors mainly like to sell products and solutions that after the first sale, generate a lot of repeat sales. This can include consumables, software upgrades, service and parts revenue. Take this into account when reviewing your value proposition. Understand "customer lifetime value" and try to possibly bring offerings to your distributors that will generate a lot of revenue and profit for many years to come to that same single end-user. These offerings will get a lot more focus (share of mind) from your distributors. Understanding the customer lifetime value well, can also help you when reviewing your distributor pricing strategy and will secure your longer term profit.

Competition information

Although I have strongly sensitized you by now on the value based selling ideas, it remains important that you understand and know as much as you possibly can about your direct competition. The more you bring arguments and uniqueness to the table, the easier you make it for your distributors to respond to customer needs and objections when they occur, the more share of mind you will gain. It contributes to that first sale speed, to that hit rate. So collect information from your existing and successful distributors. Learn how they sell against competition and share it with others. Do your "voice of customer" sessions and whatever else it takes to position your products and solutions stronger against competition. Share it with them in a format that is easy to use and easily accessible when and where needed in the sales process. This includes competition price change information, product and organizational changes.

Do not be afraid to share this with your distributors even when not really in favour of your own position. If they are professional and loyal to you, then they know how to handle this information towards their end-customers. They will prefer this over being taken by surprise themselves when talking to their next potential end-user and not knowing how to respond at that time.

Training

Next to the obvious need for regular sales contacts, training is definitely one of the remaining and important contributors to share of mind that I like to mention. Not only does it contribute to more successful sales and service of your product, but it also contributes to that generation of sparks.

Dare to think outside of the box of product training, however. Distributors in general also appreciate your help in training their team on their sales skills and even marketing skills. Not only value based selling skills but also topics like buyer profiles, sales time management are potentially valuable topics to include in your next international distributor meeting.

Marketing related topics can do some magic as well. How can distributors get more traffic on their website? What are the do's and don'ts with social media? Distributors are not marketing experts in general and will appreciate your help. Be that great company to do business with, the one that embraces their distributors. They will not forget.

I can still continue this list but rather invite you to continue the exercise yourself and to think about what else may create sparks in the brains of your distributors on a regular base. Compare it to what you do today. Earn your future slot in their minds.

Managing channel conflicts

Share of mind may be impacted by regular channel conflicts. So, learn to manage them better.

Channel conflicts with your distributors or between your distributors will be perceived as a luxury problem by some. You may believe indeed that it is better to have two parties working on a potential customer than none at all. This is of course partially true but generally leads to frustration on the side of those parties and to tension in your relationship with the distributors.

It is easier to file down the claws of a tiger than to teach a sheep how to attack.

No company can guarantee that a channel conflict will never occur. This is for the simple reason that people do business, not companies or machines. It can be tempting for some distributors to sell outside the appointed region. Sometimes end-customers themselves may insist on buying from a specific party, maybe even for an understandable reason or business history.

What matters the most to you as a vendor is to be pro-active and to avoid channel conflicts upfront. Do not assume that nobody will ever find out when you set up that one alternative channel. In today's digital world they will. And when channel conflicts occur, handle them with assertive leadership. I think it is really that simple and I will of course explain to you why that is.

HOW CHANNEL CONFLICTS ARISE

The most typical channel conflicts will evolve around the goals of the partnership, the roles of the stakeholders, the activities that are executed or the rewards for the performance that is delivered.

The conflicts may be horizontal ones. This means that they exist amongst market players at the same level, for example between distributors. Or they may be vertical conflicts. That is between vertical levels in a marketing channel. A typical example would be the relationship between wholesalers and their distributors.

Other differentiation in the types of conflicts would be the source of the conflict. We typically see channel conflicts that are induced by the vendor with e.g. direct offerings done to customers or a breach by the vendor of the granted exclusivity to the distributor. It can also be induced by the creation of a private label brand next to the regular product offering in the same market. Or it can typically also be the result of price favouring by the vendor to specific players or channels.

Another source for channel conflict induction may not be you, the vendor, but rather the distributor himself. Typical examples would be breaches of brand exclusivity by starting to sell other products next to your brand. It can be selling outside of the agreed territory or an unwanted creation of a sub-dealer network. Or it can be the result of false expectations where a distributor deliberately starts an unwanted offering of your completely new product line to the market that was not formally agreed with them yet and for which you were maybe thinking of installing a different type of distributors.

A third category are the channel conflicts that are induced by the end-users themselves. This can be on their own initiative but sometimes also pushed by the distributor that unrightfully tries to take over. I refer here mainly to unwillingness of your end-customer to work with certain distributors for performance or personal reasons.

Last but not least there is the category of channel conflicts that you induce yourself again by not setting the targets and KPIs correctly. If you have sales people working through distributors and another team in charge of private label/OEM business, then both channels may be fighting for the same end-customers. If the incentive is not – at least partially – based on their common success, then you may create unnecessary tension and fights between your own sales teams, potentially leading even to loss of confused customers.

I am not going to give you an answer for each individual situation but will try to give you an indication on how to minimize channel conflicts and how to come to a resolution in case they do happen.

AVOIDANCE AND LEADERSHIP

A first remark I like to make is that many companies assume that distributors only deal with you directly and do not interact with each other. Think again. They are in contact with each other more often than you think. They exchange information and even prices. They generally know very well what is going on and sometimes even develop a joint approach towards their supplier. Do not underestimate their network. Be honest to them and to yourself.

My second remark is that many vendors do not realize that setting up an e-commerce channel like a webshop, a sales app or other, is creating a potentially conflicting channel to your distributorships. Although technically feasible to limit access to webshops by country, it is often perceived as unfair competition by distributors if no compensation is given for sales efforts that they have potentially executed to those same online customers. So think before you launch your online channels.

Avoidance is a wonderful therapy.

– Maggie Stiefvater

Avoidance through anticipation can help you a lot. Do your homework. Be consistent in your strategy. Do not apply unjustifiable price favouritism between channels. Communicate clearly and openly. Discuss your channel strategy change plans in advance with your established channels. Turn it into a win-win situation for all parties and do not lie to your distributors about what you are doing. This will minimize the number of conflicts that you encounter. Editing strong distributor agreements, as we discussed before, is of course one of the other tools to create clarity on the expected and approved activities, on the roles and the compensations.

In case a complaint does get to your table nevertheless, the following pragmatic approach always worked best for me. On the one hand try to objectively evaluate the importance of the topic to your own business. How much will it impact your current and future business results? And do the same assessment for the side of the distributor. You may initially not care too much since you will get the deal anyway, but it may have a dramatic impact on the side of the distributor who has worked hard to get the deal (or exactly has done nothing at all and just kills it with price). Based on your professional assessment on the two axes, apply the following attitude towards the distributor that has induced the conflict situation.

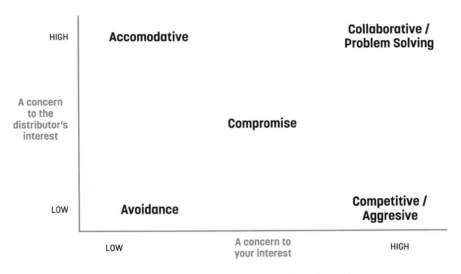

Source: Slideshare - Channel Relationship - Jigar Mehta

Leadership is the other key word. Distributors do understand that you have no full control over what every individual in your entire distributor network says or does. But they expect you to take charge and resolve issues, preferably even quickly and assertively, where needed and when they do occur. Clean the house. Your professionalism and sense of urgency, while taking the above decision matrix into consideration, will create trust on the side of your channel partners. It will again contribute to that highly needed share of mind and to the ease of mind that I referred to earlier for the distributors.

5

DEVELOPING YOUR DISTRIBUTORS

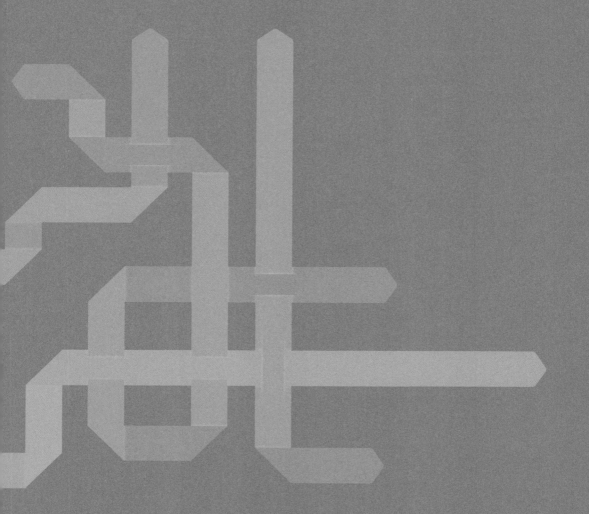

Distributors as an extension

We have defined distributors as being customers of your company as well as an extension of your organization, not only in sales but also in marketing and services. We have previously assigned your distributor account managers the very challenging job level of sales manager of a huge, international sales team which by coincidence and unfortunately are not even on your payroll and not reporting directly to you. That sales team gets their salaries and commissions paid by your local distributors. This means that your company has only very limited control over the process of their people management, over setting individual sales targets, measuring performance and definitely not over the hiring and firing of the best salespeople in your distributor's organization.

However, while treating your distributors below as the "extension of your organization", you should try to maximize your impact on the management team of your distributors as well as on their local sales and marketing team, just like you (should) do with your own team. Let us review some tools that you have available to maximize that impact.

ALIGN YOUR STRATEGIES

First, make sure that each of your key distributors understands your short and mid-term strategy that we developed in the first chapter. Communicate clearly where you want to be in the following few years (strategic plan) and how you want to get there (business plan). Which segments do you want to address and how? Which pricing and communication strategy do you want to see implemented by the distributor to support your plan (marketing plan), and more. Have your distributors, formally or at least informally, sign off on this joint strategy. Failing to align your strategy with the distributor's strategy will almost guaranteed lead to difficult discussions on targets and actual performance later on.

SET FINANCIAL TARGETS

Although some distributors do not always enjoy this part, it is vital that you agree with them on financial targets, both on an annual as even on a quarterly level as a minimum. How often did you hear the phrase: *"We know the numbers were very disappointing till now but the last quarter of the year is going to be very good, trust us"*. And then the budget does not materialize, but too late to still implement corrective actions.

Make sure the targets have sufficient level of detail by product category or segment. Underperformance in one segment, compensated with some luck in another one does not necessarily deserve a big round of applause. All segments should be analysed and evaluated separately.

Countries and industries have their typical seasonal factors and those can and should be taken into consideration when setting your quarterly targets. Sales history many times will help you in setting realistic expectations. By setting also quarterly targets you will increase your business partner's focus and create sufficient moments for performance evaluation, review of the activity plans and distributor coaching.

Goals transform a random walk into a chase.
– Mihaly Csikszentmihalyi

Keep it simple. Your target sheet may look like this example below. Preferably make it an attachment to your distributor agreement that you make reference to in the base (legal) text and review it on an annual basis, preferably before the ending of the current year. Remember from the chapter on strategy how important it is to have your homework done in case you want to have an efficient target discussion and have ambitious but achievable targets accepted by your distributor. Without sufficient market understanding, your expectations and targets may be completely off. And this may be in two directions, up and down.

FINANCIAL TARGETS 2018

MyCompany

MyDistributor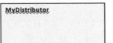

	Target 2018 350.000 €	1st Quarter (%)	2nd Quarter (%)	3rd Quarter (%)	4th Quarter (%)
Product Group 1	90.000 €	25%	25%	25%	25%
Product Group 2	150.000 €	20%	20%	30%	30%
Product Group 3	30.000 €	25%	25%	25%	25%
Product Group 4	50.000 €	10%	0%	0%	90%
Product Group 5	30.000 €	25%	25%	25%	25%

	Target 2018 350.000 €	1st Quarter €	2nd Quarter €	3rd Quarter €	4th Quarter €
Product Group 1	90.000 €	22.500	22.500	22.500	22.500
Product Group 2	150.000 €	30.000	30.000	45.000	45.000
Product Group 3	30.000 €	7.500	7.500	7.500	7.500
Product Group 4	50.000 €	5.000	-	-	45.000
Product Group 5	30.000 €	7.500	7.500	7.500	7.500
		72.500	67.500	82.500	127.500

(date)

MyCompany

....
NAME
Job Title

MyDistributor

....
NAME
Job Title

MEASURE BUSINESS PERFORMANCE

Report at least on a quarterly basis to the distributor how they performed in purchasing product from you against those targets. Some may know this themselves but most of your distributors are more focused on their own sales numbers to end-users than on their purchasing volume from you. Some will even see that information providing as a well appreciated service to them. By making this a standard reporting process, your account managers can and should follow up with the key distributors on the main deviations during their regular sales contacts.

It is indeed the role of your account management and on a less frequent base also upper management, to set up this formal contact with the distributor to understand the results and even more importantly, to agree on the plans on how to correct the results in the months to come in case of negative deviations. But also, the ones doing well can probably be pushed still to do even better with your support. Try to make these meetings a fixed moment in the contact planning. Also do not forget to congratulate your high performers and mean it. Never take their performance for granted. They will highly appreciate a little thumbs up from time to time.

The reason I stress the importance of target setting and performance measurement is not only to get and maintain focus on your products but also because sometimes partnerships do not work out as expected. Failing to set targets and to communicate on performance will make your life a lot more difficult when trying to divorce from your business partner later on. This is no different from employees who are fired but were never told that their performance was below expectation, nor given a chance to correct the situation.

Also, distributors that have worked for you for many years have developed important legal rights. Since I am not a legal expert, I will not go into details on this. But most important, discussing the termination of a distributor agreement, or at least the exclusivity of such an agreement, should never come as a surprise to your distributor but should be based on proven and continuous negative deviation from agreed targets.

INCENTIVIZE YOUR DISTRIBUTORS

Although some resistance may be experienced, particularly at the start, distributor performance can be influenced in a positive way by making your discount structure partially dependent on their performance. Or still, make a given percentage of your discount conditional, this means dependant on the achievement of business goals that were not just set by you only but "mutually" agreed upon. They not only act as a give and take between you and your distributor but they are also a nice cross-check for you on how serious the distributor is about the financial targets that were agreed upon. And of course for them it is a great incentive to make better margin still when achieving the agreed targets. This is a win-win for both parties.

One of the challenges is to find the right balance between immediate discounts at ordering date versus the year-end bonus. Of course every distributor would like to see his discount granted immediately. It creates more margin short term and there is no or at least less financial pain for the distributor if he fails to deliver the agreed financial targets. The risk is fully on your end. Of course they will all try to convince you that this is the only way they like to work.

Particularly for the ones "still taking orders but not selling anymore", as we discussed before, for the ones too strongly focused on other products than yours, this is of course the most comfortable position to be in... at your expense.

When applying a year-end bonus, that carrot hanging at the finish line will potentially make your distributors work harder in those last weeks of the business year in order to still get the incentive. Despite of hopefully a good personal relationship with your distributor, there should preferably be no exceptions to the rule. If you accept the excuses, if you do grant bonuses still when below target, then your whole system is doomed to fail. For this reason, rather have your financial department execute the calculations and communication around this, rather than your account management. This way you will support and protect them better in the sometimes unpleasant discussions.

I sometimes get asked what is the optimal incentive or percentage of bonus to be granted. Of course there is no single answer to this justified question but I tend to answer it as follows. If it hurts the distributor when failing to get the incentive, if they will be strongly disappointed and will still try to claim it for landing just short of their target, then you are probably where you should be in the mix between immediate discount and bonus.

One catch in this process of course is that your customer service and supply chain may experience a lot of year-end orders with distributors building inventory, just to achieve their targets. Next to the increased pressure on your team that is thinking already about their Christmas dinner and vacation, it may also lead to a low order intake in your next quarter. But this is just another good reason not to wait until the beginning of the business year to agree on targets with your distributors for the coming year, but do it well in time so you don't shoot yourself in the foot.

REQUEST SALES ACTIVITY PLANNING

What many vendors fail to do, is working with their distributors on a detailed Sales Activity Plan. Having a commitment from their side on financial targets is of course a good starting point, but throwing numbers at you to keep you happy is actually easy for them to do. Think about how often in your career you had an agreement on targets with your distributors and they were not met, for unjustified or sometimes even for justified reasons. But also ask yourself how often you did ask for the detailed plan that was going to support their financial target commitment. Not too often probably. Too many times companies just rely on the numbers and put their focus on the distributors that are showing lower numbers than anticipated.

A goal without a plan is just a wish.
– Antoine de Saint-Exupéry

Also here, keep it simple. More important than the format, is the process itself. Distributors that fail to share with you their detailed sales activity planning, many times just don't have one in place or do have their resources allocated to other products in their offering. Of course it is the job of your own sales and marketing team to support the distributor in developing such a plan. They also expect you to bring ideas to the table, to share success stories from other distributors, to provide marketing tools they can use, to make your product experts available to support them on that next big customer event they will put in their sales activity plan. It is all part of handling your distributors as an extension of your organization. Coach them.

Your preferred order however is for them to develop and present the plan first and for you to review it with them. And then, if needed, with your upper management you can discuss how and to what extend you will support them in the plan, what the expected ROI will be and more. Below is a simple template that could be of use to you. For each of your target segments, discuss with your individual distributors what you want to achieve. Best use the well-known "SMART" target setting principle (Simple, Measurable, Attainable, Realistic and Timeframe). On a separate sheet from the activities plan, make the time plan as well. This way it becomes a great tool for your account managers to have efficient sales meetings with your distributors. This way, again, you treat them as an extension of your organization and not just as customers that should be served whenever they want something.

Segment 1 Description	Actions / Activities What will be done for this objective?	Responsibility Who will do it?	Timeline Start & finish date	Resources Resources needed?	Challenges/Barriers Which ones?	Communication How will you communicate?	Result/Outcome Measureable outcome?	Current Status
Objective 1:								
1								
2								
3								
4								
5								
Objective 2:								
1								
2								
3								
4								
5								
Objective 3:								
1								
2								
3								
4								
5								

Sales Activity Planning 2018 - Objectives & Activities by Target Segment (Activities). COUNTRY: DISTRIBUTOR: ACTIVITIES. DATE CREATION: DATE LATEST UPDATE:

Sales Activity Planning 2018 - Objectives & Activities by Target Segment (Timing)

COUNTRY:		TIMING	DATE CREATION:
DISTRIBUTOR:			DATE LATEST UPDATE:

Segment 1 Description	Actions / Activities What will be done	Jan	Feb	Mar	Apr	May	Jun	Jul	Aug	Sep	Oct	Nov	Dec
	Objective 1:												
1	(= repetition from chart "ACTIVITIES")												
2													
3													
4													
5													
	Objective 2:												
1													
2													
3													
4													
5													
	Objective 3:												
1													
2													
3													
4													
5													

MEASURE OVERALL PERFORMANCE

I have worked with companies that have developed simple but useful distributor scoring systems which do serve as an annual and general evaluation, not only referring to financial targets, but also to their interaction with the supplier. This actually brings us back to the chapter on the distributor profile. If you have a clear profile in place of your ideal distributor, then it should not be too difficult to get such a template in place for your company and to measure the overall performance of your individual distributors. The performance indicators of course must match with your strategic priorities.

Allow me to share with you an anonymized and slightly reworked template from a company that I worked with a few years ago. It can work as a nice starting point for you. Build your own and make sure enough stakeholders in your team get involved in the final scoring.

Section		Criteria	Weight %	Score/10	Total
Sales Performance	SP1	Revenue in our Top 3 Prod Cat.	20	8,0	16,0
	SP2	Average growth past 3 years	10	6,0	6,0
	SP3	Service Profitability	10	4,0	4,0
Communication	C4	Overall communication	10	8,0	8,0
	C5	Sales Activity Planning	15	7,0	10,5
Marketing	M6	Dedicated events for our brand	10	10,0	10,0
	M7	Use of our Marketing Initiatives	5	8,0	4,0
	M8	Use of our Partner site	5	8,0	4,0
Training	T9	International Training Participation	10	10,0	10,0
Supply Chain	O10	Forecasting Accuracy	5	4,0	2,0
			100		74,5

Next to coaching your distributor (as again you do or should do with your own staff), one other objective of such template can be to reward your best distributors at for instance your next international distributor meeting. Trust me, since not companies do business with companies, but people do business with people, this will be highly appreciated by the successful business partners that do go the extra mile. Everybody wants to be up there on stage, being told in the presence of their peers that they were the best performers last year and why that was.

Note that by bringing in other parameters than revenue, every distributor, even the rookie distributor that only started working with you last year, has a chance to being rewarded and being recognized for the great work they did, for aligning and delivering on your strategic and business planning. It also allows you to perform the necessary benchmarking for each distributor against the gold standard in your company.

What gets measured, gets done. What gets measured and fed back, gets done well. What gets rewarded, gets repeated.

– John E. Jones

COACH YOUR DISTRIBUTORS

Just like you would do with your own team members, coaching will add value in developing your distributors. Your big challenge is getting the buy-in from your distributor and will largely depend on the way you do this, the timing and the attitude that you will show in the process , and the skills of your account managers.

Distributors are not waiting for paternalists to come and tell them how to run their business. But they are not waiting for despots that tell them over and over again that they are the worst students in the class either. If you have developed the right level of partnership, the mutual respect and openness, then proper coaching can help you in making your distributors understand that they are not only customers but also an extension of your organization. They are your representation in the market and should understand that is why you are entitled to coach them. You want to develop them to becoming even better business partners.

One simple approach to coaching your distributors and a good tool when preparing such a coaching sales meeting is the so-called **GROW** model, which stands for:

> **G**oal
> **R**eality
> **O**ptions (**O**bstacles)
> **W**illingness (**W**ay forward)

Goal: Where do you want the distributor to be? What do you expect from them? This is why the target setting, preferably on a quarterly base is key, as discussed above.

Reality: What is the current situation? Which business areas deviate from the expected? This is why the reporting by your financial department and commenting by your skilled account management is also crucial in the process.

Options: What is causing the gap? What are the options to correct it? This is the coaching process where based on your experience, success stories from other distributors and your own ideas, you will suggest to the distributor what can be done to correct the situation and still achieve the targets.

Willingness: What are the corrective actions? Is the distributor truly committing to this? I think this is the sometimes most challenging but also most important part of the coaching process. It is easy for distributors to state that the situation will improve. But how committed are they really? Or is it just blowing smoke to keep you happy?

Many of the tools that we discussed above, including the financial target setting, the sales activity planning, the overall performance measurement, will all serve as your barometer when preparing and having your coaching sessions with your distributors.

HAVE REGULAR SALES MEETINGS

Distributors in general do not walk away because of price or because of other very predictable reasons. They usually walk away because of a lack of attention. Attention in this case should not be translated into "always agreeing when they ask for something". It starts with connecting to them in the first place, being in touch with them, bringing solutions and support to their business success. It is about turning every contact with your distributors into an event. Regular sales meetings, regular constructive interactions with your distributors, are part of creating that level of attention. And since you cannot and should not manage all distributors with the same level of attention, prioritization and time management are of essence here. I will not go deeper into detail on account and time management since many valuable publications on this topic are available in bookstores and on the Internet. But as indicated to you already, start at least an internal distributor segmentation process in your organization if not yet in place. Prioritize.

As a closing statement to this chapter, I also hope that by now you have started to understand why I believe the role of the distributor account or sales managers to be a very demanding one. The many skills that are needed to get the most out of your distributors, turns the job into one of playing Premier League soccer. You and your distributors deserve only the best players on the job.

Satisfying your distributors

Many times by now I have tried to get you focused on your distributors as an extension of your organization. But remember that they are also your customers. This means their overall satisfaction does matter to you. You want them to work hard for you, to give you the necessary share of mind, so do not forget to check on a regular base how they enjoy working with you and for you.

MEASURE DISTRIBUTOR SATISFACTION

Just like we do (or should at least) measure direct customer satisfaction and just like you hopefully also measure your employee satisfaction from time to time, it is equally vital that the satisfaction of your distributors gets measured. Only very few companies however take the time to do so. This has several reasons. Some believe it weakens their own negotiation position, some will claim that distributors always complain by default just to put pressure on prices and to explain their underperformance. Some just don't even want to hear what the distributors think. They should just execute. So why ask?

Vulnerability is our most accurate measurement of courage.

– Brené Brown

I believe the contrary to be true. Measuring satisfaction either in a formal way like once per year or in a more informal way, e.g. through your distributor meeting reports, will actually strengthen your position and negotiation power.

On the one hand it will make you better and more appreciated as a company. If you understand what adds value to your distributors, you will maximize margin in the end. If you show interest in your distributor's satisfaction, if it measures positive on a regular base, then you have just strengthened your negotiation position next time your distributor asks you for better pricing. It will create more trust in your position as a vendor and will make you less fearful.

Remember also in this respect the difference between complaints and objections, the latter being based on perception. If your distributor expresses a perception that you may not like, try to change the perception through listening to what is meant and through proof. If they have a complaint – and I have explained the difference to you earlier – then fix it, share the information on the fix with them and get confirmation on the resolution from them. Preferably do this in writing since distributors tend to forget.

Your most unhappy customers are your greatest source of learning.
– Bill Gates

One important message again, if you measure distributor satisfaction in a formal way and you ask them about your pricing, it SHOULD show a lower score. If you score very well on this topic, then immediately increase your prices. If not mentioned by the distributor as being an issue, then without any doubt your prices are too low. This is a provocative statement indeed but absolutely true.

Although I do not believe that huge financial investments should be done for measuring distributor satisfaction, I would recommend you to bring in professionals from time to time. They usually know best how to put smart questions together, how to test the questions upfront and even more important, how to read the results correctly. External parties will also have a more objective look at the results and not jump to conclusions as you would probably do from time to time.

Now, since not all of you may immediately set up a formal distributor satisfaction measurement program after reading this book, here are some tips on what distributors like and dislike in general. The list is not exhaustive but hopefully a good starting point for you.

WHAT DISTRIBUTORS LIKE

» Distributors want you to provide all possible tools and support that help them grow their revenue and margin, not only yours (value based sales arguments, professional marketing communication tools, competition information, market trends, success stories and more).

» They want you to visit them, not to just deliver to them.
(Which refers to giving them the necessary attention in general – see chapter on share of mind.)

» They want to see the distributorship grow into a relationship.

» They want the relationship not to be static but dynamic.
(Regular product and process innovations, creative solutions to challenges, success story sharing, social media updates…)

» They want you to be proactive instead of reactive.
(Get information shared regularly on potential product or delivery issues, on expected competition activity, no surprises, anticipation…)

» They want timely response, a healthy sense of urgency.
(Never forget that many times they have been working themselves already on a solution with the end-customers without bothering you, which makes it urgent when they come and ask you for support now.)

Customers don't measure you on how hard you tried. They measure you on what you deliver.
– Steve Jobs

WHAT DISTRIBUTORS DON'T LIKE

» Distributors do not like to be disrespected.
» They dislike not being taken serious.
   (No understanding for the sometimes – not always – high urgency of their requests.)
» They dislike not being involved at all in your company strategy.
   (Even though their own strategic agenda may differ from yours sometimes indeed.)
» They want you to always be one step ahead in product expertise.
   (Sometimes they have developed more expertise on products or the industry than you – try to catch up with them.)
» They do not like you to oversell your product or services performance and then not being able to live up to the expectation.
   (Share the truth or at least do not lie, since most distributors know perfectly well how to handle bad news with their end-users.)
» They do not like to be sold to too hard as if you are the only option available.
   (Because most of the time indeed you are not.)
» They do not like instability and surprises (having a standard but reliable delivery time of e.g. two months may be appreciated more than most of the time only one and a half months and two or three times out of ten it is between three and four months. Or even worse, if you can never tell for sure.)
» They do not appreciate strong defence or not being heard when bringing issues to the table.
   (See chapter on managing objections and learn how to deal with this better.)

As a closing statement to this chapter, let me remind you of the distributor segmentation that I suggested to you. All distributors do matter. Your smallest size distributor also adds to the numbers. But, you simply do not have the time neither the resources available to please all of your distributors. So, prioritize.

Be picky with who you invest your time in. Wasted time is worse than wasted money.
– anonymous

Changing your distribution channels

One day you will want to extend your existing channel network or even replace the existing distributors with others. If you have identified and clearly reported to your existing distributors a market potential that exceeds significantly their performance and coverage, it is fair to check with them their willingness to grow their organization. Remember the GROW coaching model. If after extensive discussion and after formal evaluation and coaching, you still do not walk away with sufficient belief in performance improvement, this is the time to act.

It is in my opinion one of the toughest decisions in managing and developing distributors. What is the best time to come to this invasive decision? What will be the impact on the business if you decide to expand your channel network or terminate existing agreements? Will the new partnership bring better results at all? Is your market information maybe not correct and therefor expectations unrealistically high?

Once again I stress here the importance of doing your strategic homework first, of travelling to the respective countries, of agreeing on clear targets with your current distributors, on requesting sales activity planning to support the financial plan, on evaluating performance on a regular base and everything else that I have mentioned before. This way, any discussion with your existing distributors on the addition of other distribution channels or on terminating your current one, should not come as a complete surprise. This is no different from handling underperformance, and worst case, termination of employment contracts with your own staff. They are entitled to performance reviews and advance warning as well, don't you think?

THE PROCRASTINATION TRAP

Procrastination is the biggest problem when considering changes in the distribution network. It is a sensitive matter and fear, choosing the road of the least resistance, your sales staff potentially missing their sales bonuses and more, often drives the decision to give it another year before you or your account managers cut the wires with the current distributor.

Without any doubt your underperforming business partner will be creative and come up with a hundred reasons why they failed to achieve their targets. The targets are in such cases often claimed to have been unrealistic from the beginning. Some of the reasons given may be justified indeed. Unexpected events may have occurred. Major projects may have had a 50/50 chance only and did not materialize in the end. But unfortunately sometimes it is just an attempt from their side to extend the agreement to the longest possible until that point of no return (your notification to terminate or your expansion to more channels) has been reached.

The situation is very much comparable to the famous but controversial experiment with the frog in a kettle with boiling water. Throw a frog in boiling water and it jumps out immediately. Put the frog in tepid water and heat the water slowly. The frog will not perceive the danger and will slowly be cooked to death. This is exactly reflecting much of our standard behaviour in dealing with underperforming distributors. We tend to give it still one more shot and often loose a valuable business year this way.

THE CHALLENGES IN CHANGING CHANNELS

When you have gathered the confidence to move ahead with a change in your channel structure, you will be facing both internal and external challenges. A lot of hurdles will cross your road and strong upper management support is needed. Let me list some of the most obvious ones.

External challenges

» The need for changing your channel strategy may not be apparent to you or other team members since revenue and profit are still slowly growing. You may fail to see that huge upside potential is being missed.

» Success with a different channel approach in other parts of the world may completely fail when being copied to other countries. There is unfortunately no guarantee that the copy-paste will work elsewhere. Markets are different, business cultures differ, market trends do not necessarily take place at the same pace. And the possibilities for testing the impact are generally limited. This is again why your initial strategic homework is so important in managing and developing your distributorships.

» Already the mere announcement of your intention to change your channel approach will create turbulence in your current distributor network. Trust will be lost, even if you decide on no change after further analysis.

» End-customers, who often buy in the first place because of the relationship with the distributor and not necessarily because of your product performance, may not be willing to buy from a newly appointed local distributor.

Internal challenges

» Any start of a new or different channel means necessary readiness of your entire team to change. The current distributor will no doubt try to influence your whole organization and prove the management of your company to be wrong in their decision.

» Personal relationships have been built over time with the current distributor and these will be under pressure. Your own team might be your biggest enemy in the process of change. This includes sales, sales support, service support and logistics.
» The pioneers that were at the base of the initial distributor agreement and of the country strategy will watch the decision takers on the announced channel change with a lot of scepticism.

From my experience in going through channel change processes, I can only state the following:

» Fear is your worst decision maker.
» Try to implement your first planned channel changes in less invasive markets, gain experience and build confidence this way.
» Accept that business may and probably will be affected short term indeed and include it in your sales budget.
» If you are in upper management, take the lead yourself as well as the responsibility for the outcome of the decision.
» Remember that contractual exclusivity is one of the highest hurdles to overcome in many cases but at the same time one of your available options to changing channel strategy without already and immediately having to appoint additional channels. Discontinuing exclusivity or making it at least conditional, often proves to be the stick needed to make distributors work harder for you. Been there, done that many times myself and with success.

CONTRACT TERMINATION

In case the partnership does not show a future, contract termination may be the only option left. Or if you build contracts like I suggested it means that the next annual extension is just not going to take place. Like with your own staff that you sometimes have to separate from, a divorce from your distributor should never come as a surprise to them, in which case you would not have managed the relationship properly.

I can only stress here again that it is wise to include clauses in your distribution agreement that cover the post termination rights and obligations. Like in real life, and fortunately this statement is not based on personal experience (*thanks for sticking with me for so long already, my love*), the best is to try to manage the channel discontinuation in a professional and constructive way. Both the distributor and you will benefit from this approach. This is of course assuming that ever in the past good business has been developed between the two of you but that for good reasons you have to discontinue the relationship at this point. Fortunately, in my experience divorcing from channels does not happen continuously and would also not create the best reputation for you as a vendor to work with.

A divorce is like an amputation.
You survive but there is less of you.
– Margaret Atwood

Since most readers like happy endings to the book, I am not going to leave you with a dramatic divorce but rather with an overview of what I believe to be your twenty most important takeaways from my personal vision on distributor management and on how to get more out of your distributors in the future.

6
YOUR TWENTY
TAKEAWAYS

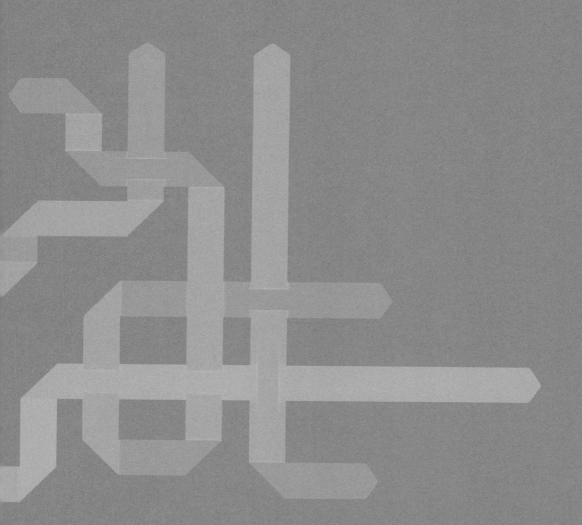

1 Failing to plan is planning to fail. Getting more out of your distributors requires professional **strategic planning** and good communication because of the many stakeholders that play a role in the next 19 takeaways below.

2 **Top sales people** are required since selling to distributors is playing Premier League soccer. Not only you but also your distributors deserve them.

3 Do not step into the **opportunism trap** when recruiting your distributors. Evaluate carefully their capability, compliance and commitment.

4 **Distributor agreements** are made for the bad days, not for the good ones. The euphoria of the new relationship should be put aside when editing a strong agreement.

5 **Perception** is the reason why distributors and end-customers (don't) buy from you. It is personal.

6 **Stop selling. Start listening**. Ask the right questions to learn what really adds value to your individual distributor.

7 **Value based selling** will help you and your distributors to stop selling against competition and will generate higher margins. First learn yourself and then educate your distributors on the basics of it.

8 Develop a **Value Proposition Canvas** not only for your end-customers but also for your distributors by understanding better their daily tasks, the gains they look for and the pains they encounter.

9 **Profit margin** is the basis of the distributor needs pyramid. If you are not "interesting" for them anymore in that perspective, they will no longer be "interested". They will still be taking orders, but they will no longer be selling (and they will not tell you).

10 **Stop selling. Start telling**. Use the power of storytelling while focusing on the "why" of what you sell and no longer on the "what" like most of your competitors do.

11 **Distributor objections and complaints** are not the same and do require a different approach. Price is and should be the most common objection in the strategic game that you can win.

12 **Distributor margin** is a compensation for the sales activities deployed by your distributors. It is not and should not be a standard percentage on your delivery price.

13 **Price negotiations are a strategic game** with your distributors in which you can lose valuable money if not preparing yourself and your team well enough for it.

14 **Be proud to be expensive**. You should be. If distributors do not object to your price, then probably you are too cheap and should increase your prices immediately.

15 **Never "give" a discount** to your distributors. Your negotiations can work a lot more to your advantage if you no longer step into the classical negotiation traps.

16 **Lack of attention** and not pricing is the main reason why distributors potentially leave you.

17 Your **real competition** is not the established brands in your industry. It is the other products and solutions that your distributor is selling.

18 **Share of wallet** and **share of mind** is the continuous fight that you are in with your distributors. Earn your spot by taking the right initiatives.

19 Distributors are **customers of your organization** but also an **extension of your organization**. You sell TO them but also THROUGH them. Measure their satisfaction but also give them clear targets and evaluate their performance. Reward them, develop them or replace them without stepping into the trap of procrastination.

20 **Training, training, training**. Whatever you have picked up from this book will have no impact in your organization unless you practice a lot and develop it into second nature, into new habits and routines.

Let me leave you with some closing business quotes that will hopefully inspire you to put at least part of the acquired knowledge into practice.

Good luck.

Everybody said it was impossible
until one person walked by that didn't know this.

– Anonymous

It always seems impossible until it's done.

– Nelson Mandela

A pessimist sees the difficulty in every opportunity.
An optimist sees the opportunity in every difficulty.

– Sir Winston Churchill

The people who are crazy enough to think
they can change the world,
are the ones who do.

– Steve Jobs